MARINA CALDARONE

Marina Caldarone is a freelance theatre and
radio drama director who has been actively
involved in actor training in the UK's leading
drama schools for the last twenty years. She
is drama director for Crying Out Loud, a
production company making training CDs for
actors. She is co-compiler of *Actions – The Actors'
Thesaurus*, also published by Nick Hern Books,
and the *Radio Active* collections of monologues
and duologues for the recorded media.

OTHER TITLES IN THIS SERIES

The Good Audition Guides

CLASSICAL MONOLOGUES FOR MEN

edited and introduced by

MARINA CALDARONE

NICK HERN BOOKS
London
www.nickhernbooks.co.uk

A NICK HERN BOOK

The Good Audition Guides:
Classical Monologues for Men
first published in Great Britain in 2006
by Nick Hern Books Limited
14 Larden Road, London W3 7ST

Introduction copyright © 2006 Marina Caldarone
Copyright in this selection © 2006 Nick Hern Books Ltd

Cover design: www.energydesignstudio.com

Typeset by Country Setting, Kingsdown, Kent, CT14 8ES
Printed and bound in Great Britain by Bookmarque,
Croydon, Surrey

A CIP catalogue record for this book
is available from the British Library

ISBN-13   978 1 85459 869 1
ISBN-10   1 85459 869 4

Thanks to Rose Bruford College Research Fund and John
Collis, who ran the Learning Resources Centre at Rose
Bruford College, which nourishes so many; Anna Linstrum
and Lindsey Bowden; and Caroline Downing.

Contents

6

8

ACKNOWLEDGEMENTS

The editor and publisher wish to thank the following for permission
to use copyright material:

Medea, Euripides, trans. David Wiles; *Hecuba*, Euripides, trans. Frank
McGuinness, Faber and Faber; *Thebans*, Liz Lochhead, after Sophocles
and Euripides, Nick Hern Books; *Bacchae*, Euripides, Kenneth McLeish,
Nick Hern Books; *Rudens*, Plautus, trans. Christopher Stace (1981),
Cambridge University Press; *Peribanez*, Lope de Vega, adapt. Tanya
Ronder, Nick Hern Books; *Life is a Dream*, Pedro Calderón de la Barca,
trans. John Clifford, Nick Hern Books; *Don Juan*, Molière, trans. Kenneth
McLeish, Nick Hern Books; *Phedra*, Racine, trans. Julie Rose, Nick Hern
Books; *Lorenzaccio* (in *Musset: Five Plays*), Alfred de Musset, trans.
Donald Watson, Methuen Publishing Ltd; *The Government Inspector*,
Nikolai Gogol, trans. Stephen Mulrine, Nick Hern Books; *An Enemy
of the People*, Henrik Ibsen, adapt. Arthur Miller, Nick Hern Books;
Ivanov, Anton Chekhov, adapt. David Hare, Methuen Publishing Ltd;
Miss Julie, August Strindberg, trans. Kenneth McLeish, Nick Hern
Books; *The Seagull*, Anton Chekhov, trans. Stephen Mulrine, Nick Hern
Books; *To Damascus Part III* (in *Strindberg: The Plays Volume II*),
August Strindberg, trans. Michael Meyer, Secker and Warburg; *Children
of the Sun*, Maxim Gorky, trans. Stephen Mulrine, Nick Hern Books.
Every effort has been made to trace all copyright holders, but if any has
been inadvertently overlooked, the publishers will be pleased to receive
information and make the necessary arrangements at the first opportunity.

Introduction

AN OPPORTUNITY, NOT A TEST ☞

Let's assume you have an audition coming up. It may be for entrance to drama school, or for your first job after training, or it could be twenty years into your career and you have been asked to show your suitability for a specific role. Whatever the circumstances, the stakes are always high, and the somewhat artificial situation is undeniably nerve-racking. You want to find a monologue that does two jobs at once: it suits your particular skills and it demonstrates your particular suitability for the job you are interviewing for.

Before you begin, it is worth remembering that the person or panel auditioning you is just as anxious . . . for you. They will want to put you at your ease, get the very best out of you, and enable you to enjoy the experience – so that they do as well. Adrenaline can be a useful energising factor, but the most valuable qualities when going into an audition are sound preparation and an ability to flex that most crucial of actors' muscles: the imagination. Dare to make brave choices in the selection and delivery of your audition piece, and you will always stand out. View your audition as an opportunity, not a test.

USING THIS BOOK ☞

The fifty speeches in this volume offer a new selection of classical monologues, divided into five distinct time periods from Ancient Greece to the 1930s. It is not an anthology of 'great speeches from dramatic literature' but, rather, a miscellany of eclectic and original monologues. Many will prove challenging; some will seem immediately unsuitable for you; others will lead you down stimulating new avenues you hadn't considered before. Most of the monologues are taken in their entirety from plays; others have been shaped and moulded from a series of separate but closely connected passages to form a coherent speech.

The monologues are arranged in chronological order, within the five time periods: Classical Greek and Roman, Elizabethan and Jacobean, French and Spanish Golden Age, Restoration and Eighteenth Century, and Nineteenth and Early Twentieth Centuries. Before each section is a short introduction to the respective period, plus some pointers that may prove interesting or useful. By and large, however, the same 'rules' for preparing your monologue apply for all time periods – whether you are delivering Ancient Greek rhetoric, Renaissance tragic verse or savage Wildean wit.

Preceding each individual monologue is a checklist of the basic information you need to know before you can begin work: *Who* is speaking; *Where*; *To whom* and *When* the character is speaking; *What has just happened* in the play to provoke the speech; *What the character wants* and some possible objectives to play. After many of the speeches is a glossary explaining less familiar words and phrases.

This checklist isn't a substitute for reading the play from which the monologue is taken. Nor is it offered as a comprehensive guide or direction on how to rehearse and present the speech. It's a starting point, a springboard, from which you need to start making your own choices, in order to achieve ownership of the monologue and your performance of it.

The important thing is to keep your performance real and truthful. Many people put too much emphasis on the notion of 'classical' text being very different and very much harder than 'contemporary' text. Yes, classical text is harder insofar as the language can be less familiar, the syntax trickier, the form less comfortable – but the heart of the work is exactly the same, albeit sometimes bigger. During the act of transformation, you will need to grow emotionally, linguistically, physically in order to speak these lines; the character remains a person inhabiting a real world – not a 'classical' one frozen in the past!

CHOOSING YOUR MONOLOGUE ☞

There are many books written on how to audition, numerous classes to take in perfecting your audition technique, and it can be easy to forget that the first, and possibly the most important, stage in the process is making your initial choice of audition material.

- You must choose a piece that plays to your personal strengths as an actor; something you know you can understand, can work with, and is within your capabilities as a performer. At the same time, you should be looking to challenge yourself and not confine yourself to any mould. Be brave!

- The speech has to 'speak' to you. You must respond to the text instinctively on some level before you can begin to take it apart. Read different speeches out loud. If you only consider a monologue from an intellectual point of view, there is a limit to what will present itself to you, but in the actual speaking of the words you will taste unexpected nuances. The power of great writing is that you can experience it on an entirely physical level as you swill the text around in your mouth.

- If you are auditioning for a specific role, you must choose one that resonates with or reflects at some level the part you are being seen for. Is it a tragic or comic piece you are auditioning for? What 'weight' is required for the role? Make a judgement and find a monologue that mirrors this dynamic. Is the character emotionally centred, forwardly energetic, or laid-back and relaxed?

- If you are auditioning for a role in a period piece, it makes sense to choose a monologue that is set in the same time period, since you will often be assessed on your ability to speak the language of that period in both a natural and an accurate way.

- Choose a speech that you are excited by, will enjoy working on, and which resonates with you as a performer and as a person. Stay instinctive.

PREPARING YOUR MONOLOGUE ☞

So you've chosen your speech and now need to prepare it for your audition. Here are some of the things you certainly should be doing, some things you might be considering, and some you should definitely be avoiding.

- Always read the play that the monologue is taken from. If you don't, you're hunting for buried treasure without thinking to consult the map. Find out what else the playwright has written, and what identifies the period specifically. This will help you form a context for the monologue and your playing of it, but also give you something to discuss with those auditioning you. An intellectually engaged actor is always an appealing one.

- Find the impulse to start the monologue. Each of the speeches in this volume appears with some suggested objectives as a starting point for you. There must always be a reason for the character to open their mouth, to start talking; there must be something they *want*. A common analogy used is this: If you dive off the diving board in the correct way, you will have a perfect flow through the air and will enter the water effortlessly. Similarly, in an audition, if you don't take a moment to clarify who you are and what you want before diving in, you'll belly flop!

- Once you have your objective/s, one useful way to proceed is to 'action' the speech. Instead of concentrating on acting moods and emotions, you find an active, transitive verb to play on each and every line or objective that helps you achieve your aim. (*Actions – The Actors' Thesaurus*, which I compiled with the actress Maggie Lloyd-Williams, offers an explanation of this widely-used system, and a thesaurus of Actioning words.)

- Consider who the speech is spoken to. It is too off-putting to look directly at the audition panel, so where will you place the person/s you are addressing. Will they move during the speech? Will you 'stage' the piece with movement and gestures, or will you remain static? All the choices you make are crucial in demonstrating your ability to inhabit a role totally.

- The language and syntax of the speech will tell you everything you need to know about the character. We are *how* we *speak*, and *what* we *say*. Look carefully at the choices the playwright has made concerning vocabulary, form and punctuation. A comma is not a full stop; a full stop is not an exclamation mark: they mean completely different things. What does it mean if a character talks rapidly, in short sentences, haltingly, and frequently punctuated, as opposed to one who talks at greater length in a much more florid sentence with rarely a punctuation mark intruding on the text? Be precise in your reading of these instructions, and follow them. Inhabit the character by allowing the text itself to lead your delivery, your breathing, your tempo. It is too often the case, when I am on an auditioning panel, that when I refer to the text of the speech that the actor in front of me is performing, I see that all the punctuation has been ignored in favour of another, generally easier, way of playing it.

- If you are being considered for a role where the character speaks mostly in verse, it would be wise to choose a monologue in verse, and show some working knowledge of how to speak it. The character expresses him or herself in verse for a reason. It's a heightened form, used when prose is not enough to convey their elevated thoughts and feelings. In a musical, a character breaks into song when spoken words are not enough. In drama, verse occurs where prose is not enough. It says a lot about a character when they move from prose to verse within a scene – or even a single speech – and vice versa. Understand and enjoy the change.

- Many of the monologues in this volume are written in iambic pentameter, the most common verse form of the Renaissance theatre. Feel your pulse now or imagine an amplified heartbeat, the short beat followed by the long – the heart pumping blood around your body does so with the rhythm of an *iamb*. So an iambic pentameter consists of a short beat, and then a long one, five times a line. De-dum de-dum de-dum de-dum de-dum. Be careful though: much verse in iambic pentameter doesn't conform rigidly to this pattern. In such cases, don't compress the beats into too regular a five-beat rhythm. The variations are important and intentional, and irregularity can reflect the character's state of mind.

- Classical text must not sound 'classical', it's in the present tense and active, and should sound as if you are speaking it today. We've all heard actors using a false, declamatory voice when performing Shakespeare. Avoid this at all costs in auditions. It is phoney and indicates an actor's ignorance of what the character is actually saying. Speak with immediacy, vitality and truth, and it will be (electrifyingly) powerful.

- The *effort* you put into preparing your monologue will be commensurate with the *effortlessness* it will appear to have in the playing. The French for 'to rehearse' is '*répéter*'. You won't go far wrong repeating and repeating your monologue, trying something different each time, keeping what you like, what 'fits', and letting go what doesn't. It is quite simple: the more fully prepared you are, the more confident you will be; the more confident you are, the more risks you will take, and the more you will 'let go' and be able to respond to any re-direction offered to you.

- However, don't overwork and overanalyse the monologue and your performance of it to the point where it becomes unnatural or forced. Ensure that all your choices are sound, based on taking appropriate time to investigate and rehearse.

PREPARING FOR YOUR AUDITION ☞

- As well as reading the play from which the monologue is taken, you should also read and research the play and the role you are auditioning for.

- Be mindful of the time limit of any speeches you are to present; two minutes is the average length for most auditions. Many of the speeches in this volume will last longer than this, but are offered here in full so you can make your own choices about which passages to play and which to cut.

- Look online for up-to-date information about those who are auditioning you. It may be that you have seen their work, which might help build a picture of what their tastes are, and give you something to talk about.

- You are your own marketing manager. Have good, professional photographs taken and then ensure that the photograph you submit captures you – not just that it *looks* like you, but that it captures your spirit and personality *energetically*. Your agent and your friends can advise you on which photos do you justice. You will lose audition opportunities otherwise, and waste the auditions you *are* invited to.

IN THE AUDITION ☞

- Wear something that the audition panel might remember you by – just wearing black is dangerous. After a day of seeing dozens of people, all of a specific physical type, it can be difficult to remember individual faces, appearances – and performances. At the same time, always dress appropriately for the part you are being considered for.

- Be in good time. A perennially late actor is a perennially unemployed one.

- Be open and positive, polite and friendly; say 'Yes' in your demeanour. That said, neediness is unattractive. Be enthusiastic but not desperate. It can be a fine line.

- Introduce yourself politely and in a professional manner. Take a moment or two to find your centre, and collect your thoughts before you begin your monologue. Always keep breathing!

- Be prepared to be asked to stop, start again, and try different approaches. It doesn't mean your interpretation was wrong; it's just that the person or panel auditioning wants to see how well you take direction and how flexible and creative you are.

AFTER THE AUDITION ☞

If you get through the audition, get recalled, or get offered the job or the drama-school place, then congratulations; the hard work paid off!

But always remember that even if you're not successful this time, you may not have lost the opportunity to work with members of the panel again. Very often a role will be offered to an actor who most closely matches the physical appearance that the director envisaged. You can do nothing about this, so don't carry the disappointment or resentment over to the next audition or opportunity.

If you are rigorous in your approach, creative in your choices, exact in your playing and comprehension of the monologue, and a pleasure to spend those few minutes with, then you will be remembered for future jobs or recommended to others. And that's something you can do everything about. So relax, start work, and enjoy the experience. Good luck!

A NOTE ON THE TEXT ☞

Many of the following monologues are assembled from successive speeches. Where dialogue has been omitted, the omission is indicated by [. . .].

Classical Greek and Roman

The Greek tragedies drew on existing myths and wrapped them up in contemporary Greek history. They are cautionary tales of how to live in what the Greeks considered a brave new world of civilisation. By contrast, the comedies are akin to situation comedies, and generally play anarchically within very established social hierarchies.

The Greeks lived in a world very different from ours today. It was savaged by war, a brutal time when life was cheap. Women were lesser citizens and slaves were people you could practically buy off a shelf. The gods controlled everything and everyone, even sometimes coming to earth to mate with mortals and breed demi-gods. Human sacrifice to the gods was considered normal, and a dialogue could be conducted with them via the Oracles, the soothsayers and the visionaries.

The dramas are huge in their sheer sweep of narrative, and graphic in their depiction of violence. Audiences would pass out at a messenger's description of a horrific death in messy, Tarantino-style detail. The plays were performed in the open air, often in enormous theatres, and with the actors (all male) wearing full face masks.

In the plays of ancient Athens and Rome, psychology is less important than story, and what characters and themes represent. When acting, it's difficult and unhelpful to play a theme or a representation, but it is important to bear your character's *function* in mind. Finding this function is subjective; there are no right or wrong choices. In his speech in this section, Polydorus could represent, for example, the innocence that is often sacrificed in war.

Don't be put off by the fact that the characters are high born, often royalty. Playwrights chose characters whom their audience would relate to as the best of themselves. The stories would be *about* them, but they would also be sufficiently removed from the characters to learn the 'lesson' of the drama and experience the cathartic power of the work. The audience is actually represented by the chorus, the commonsense voice of reasonable men (and women).

The use of masks would have fostered a highly stylised and formalised method of presentation. But today, classical plays are performed in all manner of different styles: epic, domestic, naturalistic or broadly comic. The monologues that follow here would serve a whole variety of differing presentational styles.

Medea

Euripides (431 BC), *trans. David Wiles*

WHO ☞   *Jason, late 20s plus.*

WHERE ☞   *Corinth: an open space.*

TO WHOM ☞   *Medea, his ex-wife.*

WHEN ☞   *A distant and mythical past.*

WHAT HAS JUST HAPPENED ☞ *Jason is married to Medea – they have two small sons. She is high born, from Colchis: she followed Jason as he came through there looking for the Golden Fleece. They recently escaped the Island of Iolkos after Medea tricked the daughters of King Pelias into killing their father and were thankfully embraced as political refugees by the Corinthians. However, Jason has fallen in love with the daughter of King Creon of Corinth, and he has left his family to be with her. They are getting married the following morning. Medea is devastated and humiliated; she is beside herself with grief and loss and has just been given twenty-four hours to leave Corinth, with her sons. The King is scared of her – she has a fearsome reputation as a meddler with witchcraft. Jason has just heard of the edict deporting her, and is furious, as he now loses contact with his sons. He blames her volatility. Here he confronts her.*

WHAT HE WANTS/OBJECTIVES TO PLAY ☞

- *To portray himself as a rational man, attempting to do the best thing for his family – including Medea.*

- *To belittle the sacrifices Medea has made to be with him.*

- *To rise above her madness and ranting without losing his dignity.*

- *To get her to leave the children behind – ultimately for her own benefit.*

- *To get her to respond with obedience by talking to her like a child and patronising her.*

NOTE ON TEXT ☞ *This translation is currently unpublished but readers are encouraged to find alternative versions in order to read the full play. A very readable and faithful translation by Kenneth McLeish and Frederic Raphael is published in Nick Hern Books' Drama Classics series.*

Jason

❝ Your outburst has meant being thrown out of the country.
I don't mind personally.
You are free to tell everyone that Jason is the scum of the earth.
But to go insulting the government!
You've really got off lightly with deportation.
I have been trying to soothe the King's feelings,
Asking for you to stay.
But you stupidly persisted, you and your treasonous utterances.
So you'll be deported.
Nevertheless I am not lacking in concern,
And have come to see to your interests, Medea.
So that you and the children will not be short of money or
     in need.
Exile is a troublesome business.
You may hate me,
But it's not in me to think badly of you [. . .]

It was an erotic entanglement that obliged you to protect me,
And I'll spare you the graphic details.
Thank you for services rendered.
But as for saving my life,
I think you got from me more than you gave.
Now the evidence.
To start with, I brought you from outlandish parts
To live in Greece, and learn about morality,
How to resolve problems by law and not by physical force.
Greece recognised your intelligence and gave you due credit.
If you'd lived at the end of the earth, no one would know
     of you.
I would have no interest in personal wealth

Or a voice more musical than Orpheus,
If I didn't have recognition.
That concludes my side of the story.
Remember you started this conversation.
As for your attack on my marriage into royalty,
Let me demonstrate – (a) that it's intelligent,
(b) that it's sensible, and (c) that it's
Doing you and my children a favour.
Please don't interrupt.
When I came here from Iolkos,
Given all the difficulties of my situation,
What greater piece of luck could I have had
As a refugee, than to marry the king's daughter?
It wasn't, as you intimate, through physical dissatisfaction
    with yourself
That I became smitten with a second woman,
Nor a desire with someone for increased fertility – we've
enough children, I've no complaints –
But, and this is the central point,
In order that we could live better and want for nothing,
Aware as I am that friends turn their back on paupers.
I want to bring up my children as they're entitled,
And to father some more, who'll be brothers to yours,
And to draw families together for their mutual advantage.
What benefit are children to you?
I could assist those now with us through the addition of more.
Isn't this sound thinking?
You wouldn't deny it, if it weren't for the sexual aspect.
You women are completely satisfied,
But if the physical side goes wrong,
That's the end of the *entente cordiale*. 〝

GLOSSARY

Orpheus – the fabled musician whose songs lured birds from the trees
Entente cordiale friendly understanding

Hecuba

Euripides (c. 424 BC), *trans. Frank McGuinness*

WHO ☞   *Polydorus, ghost of the dead son of Hecuba.*

WHERE ☞   *The shoreline of the ocean, Greece.*

TO WHOM ☞   *The audience.*

WHEN ☞   *Set around 400 BC.*

WHAT HAS JUST HAPPENED ☞   *Hecuba and her daughter, Polyxena, together with large numbers of Trojan women, are prisoners of war after the Greeks' victory at the first Great War between the east and west. Hecuba's son had been left with a friend for protection, but as we hear in his speech, that friend has murdered him for his knowledge of the money hidden by his father Priam.*

WHAT HE WANTS/OBJECTIVES TO PLAY ☞

- *To lull the audience into what sounds like a story but what is actually an indictment of what the world is. The horrors he describes are the new norm in this world.*

- *To get the listener to support the Trojans, to be emotionally active to balance the fact that he can only be a passive teller of the tale. He is dead and so cannot help.*

- *To be buried with all due rights so that he can find eternal rest.*

- *To reveal himself to his mother in as gentle a way as possible.*

Polydorus

❝ I am Polydorus, son of Hecuba.
Priam is my father.
I am dead.
I come from that darkness –
The abyss, the gates of godless hell.

Son of Hecuba,
Priam is my father –
He sent me from Troy,
Besieged by the Greeks;
Fearing the fall of Troy,
He secreted me
Away to Thrace,
To the home of his friend,
Polymestor, old friend
Who ploughs that fertile land,
Who rules its horsemen.
My father hid with me
A hoard of gold.
Should the walls of Troy fall,
His children would not want.
I was Priam's youngest son.
The runt with no spear,
The arm without armour,
That's why he sped me
In secret from my home.

The war went our way –
The city was not shafted –
The towers did not break,
Troy, towers of Troy,
And my brother Hector,
He won the lucky day.
Then I was the pet, the pup,
Fawned on by my father's friends,
Honoured guest in Thrace,
Though my pampered heart ached.
Then, Troy fell, destroyed,
And so too did Hector.
My father's hearth smashed,
Razed to the ground,
He too turned to dust,
At the altars our gods built,
Slaughtered by Achilles' son,
His dirty blood hand.

My father's friend killed me,
His friend killed myself.
He did it for the gold,
I had none to defend me.
He kicked my corpse,
Kicked it into the ocean.
He did it for the gold,
To keep it in his house.
Times I lie on the shore,
Times I roll in the sea's swell,
The water's ebb and flow,
None to mourn me,
Nor to bury me.
Now I leave my corpse,
I fly above Hecuba,
My mother – three days,
The same days since she,
My heart-sore mother,
Came to this alien land,
From Troy – Troy.
The Greeks and their ships,
They sit idle in Thrace.
Achilles' ghost has appeared
Above his tomb.
He's halted the army's sails
As they steered the sea to home.
He desires my sister,
He asks for Polyxena,
He wants her as his sacrifice,
Her life for his honour.
He'll get what he craves –
His cronies will see to that.
My sister will die today.
That is sealed and settled.
My mother shall look down,
She'll see two dead children,
Her son and doomed daughter.
The broken waves carry me

To land at a servant's feet –
That way I will be buried.
I asked a favour from the dead,
From those who rule over them.
Free me into my mother's hand,
Let her put me in the earth.
That's what I want – what I'll get.
But I'll back away from her,
Get out of Hecuba's way.
She's seen me somehow –
She's frightened,
She who was queen,
Housed in a palace.
Now your days are bondage,
You are last who once was first,
Your good fortune's soured to bad,
For a god devours you. **"**

GLOSSARY

Thrace kingdom ruled by Polymestor. Located northeast of Greece,
    just opposite Troy at the entrance to the Black Sea
Achilles King of Phthia, greatest warrior of Greece

Thebans

Liz Lochhead (2003),
after Sophocles and Euripides (*5th century* BC)

WHO ☞   *Polyneikes, 20s* (*pronounced Polly-*NIGH-*keys*).

WHERE ☞   *In the open in Thebes.*

TO WHOM ☞   *His mother, acting as arbitrator, and brother, in the presence of the chorus.*

WHEN ☞   *In a distant and mythical past.*

WHAT HAS JUST HAPPENED ☞   *It has been ten years since Oedipus blinded himself and went into exile after discovering he had killed his own blood father, and married his own mother, Jokasta. His twin sons Polyneikes and Eteokles had agreed to jointly take charge of Thebes, on an alternating annual basis, the first occupamncy decided on the toss of a coin. But it hasn't happened. Eteokles has refused to hand back the Kingship to his brother when it is his rightful turn. And they have become arch enemies. Polyneikes has returned to Thebes from Argos with his father-in-law King Adrastos' army to reclaim the throne, by killing his brother if needs be. Jokasta has been imploring them to look each other in the eye, to remember they are brothers. The speech is laid out very deliberately as poetry by the writer; enjoy this as it dictates the speech patterns of the character, the lay-out is how the character thinks. But ensure in your delivery it does not sound like poetry, but that it sounds real.*

WHAT HE WANTS / OBJECTIVES TO PLAY ☞

- *To state his case calmly, irrefutably, dispassionately.*

- *To win support, by proving himself fair and just — in comparison with his brother who has reneged on his word.*

- *To let his family know that this deception has removed all fraternal ties.*

- *To demonstrate this 'politics in action' for the benefit of the on-looking Theban chorus.*

- *To resolve the situation without taking arms against his own country and people.*

Polyneikes

" truth is a simple thing   no gloss necessary
only lies and injustice need
to be dressed up in fancy arguments
all I wanted was fairness and   frankly
I expected it
So   having lost the toss of the coin   I went off whistling
into voluntary exile   for one year
I'd be back   I'd take my turn

I must explain to you
in case you have forgotten   Thebans
we had a deal between us
I and Eteokles here
my own twin brother   can you believe it?

Kreon   our uncle
during our childhood   ruled as regent
and well   and fairly
but now we had come of age
it was time for us to take the reins

it was agreed that   turn about   rotating every year
we'd power-share
this would save our city from any threat
of tyranny or totalitarianism

but here's what happened
he   who swore his solemn oath   reneged
will keep no part of his promise
he won't stand down
he clings to power and keeps hold
of my share in this state

even now I am prepared   on one condition
that I get what's mine   no more no less

to send my army away from Thebes
take power for the duration of no more
than my appointed turn   to transfer it
back to him when my time's up
trust him to have learned his lesson
I will not destroy my own city   or invade it
not unless simple justice is denied me
gods   are you watching?
you know my country has been stolen from me
I know you won't let it happen

this is how it is in plain-speak   mother
irrefutable
surely you know the truth when you hear it? **99**

Bacchae

Euripides (c. 405 BC), trans. Kenneth McLeish

WHO ☞ *Pentheus (pronounced* PEN-*thyoos), son of Princess Agave and ruler of Thebes.*

WHERE ☞ *Thebes. An open space before Pentheus' royal palace.*

TO WHOM ☞ *Two old men, Teiresias and Kadmos, and the chorus of Bacchae. In the presence of the Royal Guards.*

WHEN ☞ *A myth from the real, if distant, past. Like our stories from Arthurian legend, they were part historical and part supposition.*

WHAT HAS JUST HAPPENED ☞ *Dionysos, god of wine and fertility, has returned to Thebes, seeking revenge for having been rejected when he was born, the doubt being that his father was not Zeus, as first believed. Disguised, he begins his plan by possessing the women of Thebes, sending them dancing on the mountaintop of Cithaeron. A chorus of female worshippers (also called Bacchantes or Maenads) have entered singing and dancing in honour of Dionysos, and the ancient, blind prophet Teiresias and Pentheus' grandfather, Kadmos, both of whom are also dressed as followers of the god, follow them. It is as they are describing how wondrous this worship makes them feel, that King Pentheus enters. Pentheus is a powerful King, but also an arrogant man, a sceptic who believes Bacchic rites are a mere cover for sensual indulgence and so is determined to suppress them, by force if necessary. Therefore he is furious to discover that while he has been out of town the women have been hoodwinked in such a manner by a 'pretty boy', a charlatan. He has arrested and imprisoned them and intends to do the same to the mysterious stranger who has encouraged such forbidden worship.*

WHAT HE WANTS/OBJECTIVES TO PLAY ☞

- *To reinstate his authority in the face of such potential opposition in the form of this 'golden boy'.*

- *To ridicule the old men, publicly.*

- *To challenge this particular God, who he believes to be a false one in this Greek world.*

- *To vent his rage for all to witness against what he believes is a ridiculous stunt.*

- *To protect his people from the threat of an overwhelming and irrational outside force.*

Pentheus

" As soon as I leave the city, trouble flares!
Some . . . epidemic of nonsense invades all Thebes.
They're leaving home, the women, skipping to the woods,
Tripping off to the hills in bogus ecstasy!
They're dancing in homage to the latest fad –
Dionysos, whoever he may be! They say there's more:
Wine-jugs, brimming beside the dancers' feet,
Our women slipping off on the quiet, one by one,
To whore with men. Divine service, they call it;
Priestesses they say they are; it's holy work.
They worship lust, not God.
As many as I found, I rounded up and jailed.
Guards; chains; the cells are crammed.
Some got away, I'll hunt them down.
Away in the hills – my own mother, Agave,
Her sisters, Ino, Autonoe –
I'll soon have them in irons as well.
This nonsense will stop, and smartly.
They say some stranger came smarming into Thebes –
Some magician, some fancy-man from Lydia –
Golden curls, perfumed ringlets, bangs –
Sex dancing in his eyes. A charmer!
They say he's at it with the girls,
Dangling his mysteries all day, all night.
I'll have him. I'll have him here, inside.
Thyrsos-waving! Tossing his lovely locks!

I'll have his head.
They say he's calling Dionysos God –
Stitched up by Zeus in his own royal thigh.
Dionysos! He was charred by a thunderbolt –
His mother too, for slandering Zeus
And saying he slept with her. Blasphemy!
Humbug! Whoever he is, he's earned the noose.

Oh look, another miracle!
Teiresias the star-gazer, in a dappled skin,
And my own grandfather beside him,
Playing Bacchants with their little sticks!
I'm sorry, granddad, it's embarrassing –
Men of your age losing what wits they had.
Unwind that ivy. Give me that stick.
Your idea, presumably, Teiresias?
New gods drum up new trade?
Read the future in some feathered guts
Then burn the bird for God? For cash!
I indulge your age, old man. If you were younger – chains,
Like all the rest of them. You encouraged these . . .
These orgies. Women and wine don't mix.
Women and wine! What good ever came from that? 99

GLOSSARY

bangs fringes of hair
thyrsos (pronounced THUR-soss) a ceremonial pine branch, carried by
    devotees of Dionysos
Agave pronounced A-ga-veh
Autonee pronounced OW-TO-no-eh
Lydia pronounced LID-ya
feathered guts one form of prophecy involved the scrutiny of the
    innards of birds
stitched up by Zeus in his own royal thigh . . . charred by a thunderbolt
    Dionysos's mother Semele was destroyed by lightning by his father
    Zeus, the king of the gods, who thereafter stored the embryo in his
    own thigh.

Rudens

Plautus (c. 200 BC), trans. Christopher Stace

WHO ☞   *Gripus, a fisherman and slave of the elderly Athenian Daemones. Any age.*

WHERE ☞   *On the sea shore.*

TO WHOM ☞   *The audience and to the Gods.*

WHEN ☞   *Contemporary with authorship.*

WHAT HAS JUST HAPPENED ☞ *This is the first time we meet Gripus, he has just had a successful and heavy catch – a trunk, which he assumes will be filled with treasure!*

WHAT HE WANTS/OBJECTIVES TO PLAY ☞

- *To give praise to Neptune, God of the Sea for his safe return and for his extraordinary catch of a trunk.*

- *To preach his philosophy of 'work hard and just rewards will follow'.*

- *To demonstrate his eloquence, his natural capacity for elevated verse in the first part, before returning to his normal parlance.*

Gripus

❝ To Neptune, dweller in the salt abodes
     Of fishes in the untrodden sea,
High praise and hearty thanks I give
     For treatin' me so handsomely!
For Neptune from 'is vast domain
     Dispatched me 'omeward safe and sound,
Me boat leak-free in a stormy sea,
And what a remarkable fish I've found!
It's a strange sort of monster 'e cast in me net,
But the richest catch I'm ever likely to get!

I'm weighed down to the ground
With the treasure I've found!
It's incredibly lucky the way
Me fishin' trip turned out today –
Not a scale not a fin did me fishin' bring in,
Just this 'ere – all the rest got away!
I leapt from me bed at the dead of night
   At the thought of the money I'd make;
I put business before a comfortable snore
   Fer me and me master's sake.
I'd determined to sail in a force eight gale,
   Not a thought fer meself I gave
And by risking disaster earn cash fer me master,
And do a good turn fer 'is slave!

Yes – a lazy man's not worth a damn! I never could stand lazy
people. A man's gotta rise with the lark if 'e wants to keep to
schedule with 'is chores. He's worse than useless if 'e waits
till 'is master turns 'im out of bed to go to work. People who
love their sleep can rest assured – of no money and a load of
trouble! Take me – because I've been up and doin' I've found
a way to be idle fer the rest of me life! **99**

Elizabethan and Jacobean

There is no such thing as 'Shakespearian acting', or 'speaking', nor a single 'correct' approach to the work or the words. The work of Shakespeare and his contemporaries is open for constant re-interpretation and re-investigation, and has been produced in as many ways as there have been productions. Any different version will work if the performances are real, and the world created is real.

A recent production of *Romeo and Juliet* by the Icelandic theatre company Vesturport situated the play in a circus ring. The actors playing Romeo and Juliet were trapeze artists conducting every moment of their intricate courtship, with all its linguistic layering and complexities, whilst flying through the air above the heads of the audience. It was a world away from more traditional productions but still beautiful, profoundly moving and true.

The second half of Elizabeth I's reign and the early years of James I's marked an exciting and innovative time for British theatre. One of the key influences was the building of a new kind of playhouse, an open-air amphitheatre. One of the best known of several in Elizabethan London was the Globe, a full-scale working replica of which can be visited today on the South Bank close to its original site. This theatre had an enormous creative and literary influence on the plays written for it. The size of the space necessitated 'big' writing, and the themes were for all people – from the illiterate groundlings who would stand in the yard to watch the play to those better educated and richer who would sit on the various levels. The work was received at various levels too; encouraging writing in which every word is crucial and carefully chosen, and nothing is arbitrary.

In order to release the meaning of these mighty lines, the modern actor must be able to paraphrase each sentence accurately, and play the intentions within. If you break the thoughts up, in an effort to savour each word, you may lose the flow of the sentence's thought and rhythm. Know what you're saying and so will your audience.

In the original productions there were no sets or lighting effects. Everything was to be created in the audience's imagination. So more than in any other genre or era of writing, you have to be able to *visualise* what you are saying, in order that the audience might see it too.

Henry VI, Part Three

William Shakespeare (1592)

WHO ☞	*King Henry, late 30s plus.*	
WHERE ☞	*Daybreak on the field of battle.*	
TO WHOM ☞	*The audience.*	
WHEN ☞	*30 December 1460.*	

WHAT HAS JUST HAPPENED ☞ *The Duke of York with the Earl of Warwick, have stormed the now empty palace in London and taken the throne. King Henry VI enters and York demands the crown. The King tells York that he and his heirs may have the crown after he, Henry, dies a natural death. York agrees. Queen Margaret, angry with her husband for his decision, divorces herself from him, and with her son, Prince Edward, leaves to join the revolting armies of the nobles. At Sandal Castle, York is convinced that his oath to not harm Henry is voided since a magistrate wasn't present when sworn. York plans to attack Henry. However Queen Margaret arrives with 20,000 men and York still intends to fight, though he and his uncles only have 5,000 men. The battle of Wakefield ensues. King Henry is alone on the battlefield having been sent away from the action by his wife and commanders. He is lost in his role as King, and we hear his innermost longings – for the simple life.*

WHAT HE WANTS/OBJECTIVES TO PLAY ☞

- *To be at peace with himself.*

- *To enjoy this moment's solace in his life, marvelling at the perfect balance within the natural world.*

- *To experience what it must be to have a simple life, all mapped out, with no real pressures, to be a shepherd for a moment.*

- *To be understood and respected and to be able to trust in others.*

- *To teach the audience what true riches are.*

King Henry

❝ This battle fares like to the morning's war,
When dying clouds contend with growing light,
What time the shepherd, blowing of his nails,
Can neither call it perfect day nor night.
Now sways it this way like a mighty sea
Forc'd by the tide to combat with the wind.
Now sways it that way like the selfsame sea
Forc'd to retire by fury of the wind.
Sometime the flood prevails, and then the wind;
Now one the better, then another best –
Both tugging to be victors, breast to breast,
Yet neither conqueror nor conquerèd.
So is the equal poise of this fell war.
Here on this molehill will I sit me down.
To whom God will, there be the victory.
For Margaret my queen, and Clifford, too,
Have chid me from the battle, swearing both
They prosper best of all when I am thence.
Would I were dead, if God's good will were so –
For what is in this world but grief and woe?
O God! Methinks it were a happy life
To be no better than a homely swain.
To sit upon a hill, as I do now;
To carve out dials quaintly, point by point,
Thereby to see the minutes how they run:
How many makes the hour full complete,
How many hours brings about the day,
How many days will finish up the year,
How many years a mortal man may live.
When this is known, then to divide the times:
So many hours must I tend my flock,
So many hours must I take my rest,
So many hours must I contemplate,
So many hours must I sport myself,
So many days my ewes have been with young,
So many weeks ere the poor fools will ean,

So many years ere I shall shear the fleece.
So minutes, hours, days, weeks, months and years,
Pass'd over to the end they were created,
Would bring white hairs unto a quiet grave.
Ah, what a life were this! How sweet! How lovely!
Gives not the hawthorn bush a sweeter shade
To shepherds looking on their seely sheep
Than doth a rich embroider'd canopy
To kings that fear their subjects' treachery?
O yes, it doth – a thousandfold it doth.
And to conclude, the shepherd's homely curds,
His cold thin drink out of his leather bottle,
His wonted sleep under a fresh tree's shade,
All which secure and sweetly he enjoys,
Is far beyond a prince's delicates,
His viands sparkling in a golden cup,
His body couchèd in a curious bed,
When care, mistrust, and treason waits on him. **99**

GLOSSARY

chid me from scolded me away from
thence from there
homely swain humble peasant
dials sun-dials
ean give birth
seely simple
curds dairy products
wonted accustomed
delicates luxury goods
viands foodstuffs

Doctor Faustus

Christopher Marlowe (1592)

WHO ☞   *Dr Faustus is a talented German scholar, who has learned everything he can learn by conventional academic means. 40s plus.*

WHERE ☞   *In Faustus' quarters, Germany.*

TO WHOM ☞   *Himself, though appealing to God and the Devil.*

WHEN ☞   *Contemporary with the authorship.*

WHAT HAS JUST HAPPENED ☞   *Twenty-four years ago Dr Faustus turned to magic; he learned the basics of Black Arts and summoned the Devil in the form of Mephistophiles. He sold his soul in exchange for twenty-four years of total power with Mephistophiles as his servant, and with Books that would enable him to achieve his every will, through magic. His twenty-four years are up and he is in the final hour. He has conjured a spirit in the form of Helen of Troy to comfort him in his last days, but is still suffering horribly as he knows he is about to be abandoned to eternal damnation. The gates of hell actually open for him as indicated in his text, as he begs God and the Devil for leniency, to no avail.*

WHAT HE WANTS/OBJECTIVES TO PLAY ☞

- *To redeem himself.*
- *To halt the passing of time.*
- *To be put out of his agony of waiting for the end.*
- *To resist his fate.*
- *To make a final plea-bargain to God.*
- *To appeal to the natural order of goodness to save him.*
- *To affirm his faith in the eyes of God.*

Dr Faustus

66 *The clock strikes eleven.*

Ah Faustus,
Now hast thou but one bare hour to live,
And then thou must be damn'd perpetually.
Stand still, you ever-moving spheres of heaven,
That time may cease and midnight never come.
Fair nature's eye, rise, rise again, and make
Perpetual day; or let this hour be but
A year, a month, a week, a natural day,
That Faustus may repent and save his soul.
O lente, lente, currite noctis equi!
The stars move still, time runs, the clock will strike.
The devil will come, and Faustus must be damn'd.
O, I'll leap up to my God; who pulls me down?
See, see, where Christ's blood streams in the firmament.
One drop would save my soul, half a drop. Ah, my Christ –
Rend not my heart for naming of my Christ;
Yet will I call on him – O spare me, Lucifer!
Where is it now? 'Tis gone: and see where God
Stretcheth out his arm, and bends his ireful brows!
Mountains and hills, come, come and fall on me,
And hide me from the heavy wrath of God.
No, no?
Then will I headlong run into the earth:
Earth, gape! O no, it will not harbour me.
You stars that reign'd at my nativity,
Whose influence hath allotted death and hell,
Now draw up Faustus like a foggy mist
Into the entrails of yon labouring cloud,
That when you vomit forth into the air
My limbs may issue from your smoky mouths,
So that my soul may but ascend to heaven.

The watch strikes.

Ah, half the hour is past: 'twill all be past anon.
O God, if thou wilt not have mercy on my soul,

Yet for Christ's sake, whose blood hath ransom'd me,
Impose some end to my incessant pain:
Let Faustus live in hell a thousand years,
A hundred thousand, and at last be sav'd.
O, no end is limited to damnèd souls!
Why wert thou not a creature wanting soul?
Or why is this immortal that thou hast?
Ah, Pythagoras' metempsychosis – were that true,
This soul should fly from me, and I be chang'd
Unto some brutish beast:
All beasts are happy, for when they die,
Their souls are soon dissolv'd in elements;
But mine must live still to be plagued in hell.
Curs'd be the parents that engender'd me:
No, Faustus, curse thyself, curse Lucifer,
That hath deprived thee of the joys of heaven!

The clock striketh twelve.

It strikes, it strikes! Now, body, turn to air,
Or Lucifer will bear thee quick to hell.

Thunder and lightning.

O soul, be changed into little water drops,
And fall into the ocean, ne'er be found.

Enter the Devils.

My God, my God, look not so fierce on me!
Adders and serpents, let me breathe awhile!
Ugly hell, gape not! Come not, Lucifer!
I'll burn my books – ah, Mephistophiles! 99

GLOSSARY

O lente, lente, currite noctis equi! 'Run slowly, slowly, you horses of the
    night!': from Ovid's *Amores* (in the context of a night of sexual bliss)
Pythagoras' metempsychosis the Ancient Greek theory of the
    transmigration of souls (whereby human souls might reincarnate as
    animals)
quick alive

The Two Gentlemen of Verona

William Shakespeare (c. 1594)

WHO ☞ *Lance, the clownish servant of Proteus, a Veronese gentleman. Late teens, 20s plus.*

WHERE ☞ *A street in Verona.*

TO WHOM ☞ *The audience.*

WHEN ☞ *Contemporary with authorship.*

WHAT HAS JUST HAPPENED ☞ *Lance is not involved with the plot of this play, though his stories illustrate the themes of the plot. He has had to leave his family in order to travel to Milan with his master Proteus, but Crab his dog, much to his consternation, has shown no distress at his departure.*

WHAT HE WANTS/OBJECTIVES TO PLAY ☞

- *To share with the audience how let down he feels by Crab, who has no strength of feeling.*

- *To paint the picture of his home-leaving as specifically and as romantically as possible. He takes great pride in his abilities as a story-teller.*

- *To cheer himself up in the telling of the story.*

Lance

66 Nay, 'twill be this hour ere I have done weeping. All the kind of the Lances have this very fault. I have received my proportion, like the prodigious son, and am going with Sir Proteus to the Imperial's court. I think Crab, my dog, be the sourest-natured dog that lives. My mother weeping, my father wailing, my sister crying, our maid howling, our cat wringing her hands, and all our house in a great perplexity, yet did not this cruel-hearted cur shed one tear. He is a stone, a very pebble-stone, and has no more pity in him than a dog. A Jew would have wept to have seen our parting. Why, my grandam, having no eyes, look you, wept herself blind at my parting. Nay, I'll show you the manner of it. This shoe is my father. No, this left shoe is my father. No, no, this left shoe is my mother. Nay, that cannot be so, neither. Yes, it is so, it is so, it hath the worser sole. This shoe with the hole in it is my mother, and this my father. A vengeance on't, there 'tis. Now, sir, this staff is my sister, for, look you, she is as white as a lily and as small as a wand. This hat is Nan our maid, I am the dog. No, the dog is himself, and I am the dog. O, the dog is me, and I am myself. Ay, so, so. Now come I to my father: 'Father, your blessing.' Now should not the shoe speak a word for weeping. Now should I kiss my father. Well, he weeps on. Now come I to my mother. O that she could speak now, like a moved woman. Well, I kiss her. Why, there 'tis. Here's my mother's breath up and down. Now come I to my sister. Mark the moan she makes. – Now the dog all this while sheds not a tear nor speaks a word. But see how I lay the dust with my tears. **"**

GLOSSARY

proportion i.e. 'portion': the proper inheritance of . . .
the prodigious son i.e. the Prodigal Son (Luke 15, 11–32)
grandam grandmother
sole a pun on 'soul'

Edward III

William Shakespeare (1595)

WHO ☞ *Lodowick, King Edward III's Secretary, anything from mid 20s.*

WHERE ☞ *Inside Roxborough Castle.*

TO WHOM ☞ *The audience.*

WHEN ☞ *1340s – during the Hundred Years War between France and England.*

WHAT HAS JUST HAPPENED ☞ *Edward has just arrived at Roxborough Castle, home of the Countess of Salisbury, to prevent an attack by the King of Scotland who has threatened to capture it. War is declared between the two countries. The Countess, whose husband is away fighting with England against France, is so very grateful to Edward that she persuades him to stay the night and to treat the place as his own. Lodowick knows his employer well, and observing how he is with the Countess, he knows Edward has fallen for her and that there is a drama afoot.*

WHAT HE WANTS/OBJECTIVES TO PLAY ☞

- *To point out the difference between the two of them – the Countess's modesty as compared to the King's shameful behaviour; her 'tender modest shame' and his 'red immodest shame'.*

- *To alert the audience that Edward's infatuation and dotage in the Countess does not augur well and may well have political consequences.*

Lodowick

❝ I might perceive his eye in her eye lost,
His ear to drink her sweet tongue's utterance,
And changing passions like inconstant clouds,
That rack upon the carriage of the winds,

Increase and die in his disturbèd cheeks.
Lo, when she blush'd, even then did he look pale,
As if her cheeks by some enchanted power
Attracted had the cherry blood from his;
Anon, with reverent fear when she grew pale,
His cheek put on their scarlet ornaments,
But no more like her oriental red
Than brick to coral, or live things to dead.
Why did he then thus counterfeit her looks?
If she did blush, 'twas tender modest shame,
Being in the sacred presence of a king;
If he did blush, 'twas red immodest shame,
To vail his eyes amiss, being a king.
If she look'd pale, 'twas silly woman's fear,
To bear herself in presence of a king;
If he look'd pale, it was with guilty fear,
To dote amiss, being a mighty king.
Then Scottish wars farewell, I fear 'twill prove
A ling'ring English siege of peevish love.
Here comes his highness walking all alone. **,,**

GLOSSARY

rack upon the carriage of are driven along by
anon immediately
oriental of daybreak
vail his eyes amiss lower his eyes, look away
silly simple
peevish temperamental

King John
William Shakespeare (1596)

WHO ☞ *Arthur, Duke of Brittany, Prince of England and young nephew of King John. Late teens/20s.*

WHERE ☞ *In a place of confinement, England.*

TO WHOM ☞ *Hubert, and Hubert's fellow executioners.*

WHEN ☞ *1201.*

WHAT HAS JUST HAPPENED ☞ *John has usurped Arthur's crown as the play opens. Arthur is the son of John's eldest recently deceased brother. A defenceless boy, Arthur is supported by King Philip of France (Arthur's mother is the French Duchess of Brittany) and the Archduke of Austria, who go to war with England. Arthur is captured and taken to England in the custody of Hubert, who is instructed to kill him. However, Hubert grows fond of his prisoner and cannot bring himself to carry out his orders, instead resigning himself to blinding the boy.*

WHAT HE WANTS/OBJECTIVES TO PLAY ☞

- *To call upon their friendship, the kindnesses shown, to save his life.*
- *To reiterate his innocence.*
- *To soften Hubert, to appeal to his sense of justice through gentle and respectful non-confrontational tactics.*

Prince Arthur

❝ Must you with hot irons burn out both mine eyes?

[HUBERT. Young boy, I must.
PRINCE ARTHUR.   And will you?
HUBERT.   And I will.]

Have you the heart? When your head did but ache,
I knit my handkerchief about your brows,

The best I had, a princess wrought it me,
And I did never ask it you again;
And with my hand at midnight held your head,
And like the watchful minutes to the hour,
Still and anon cheer'd up the heavy time,
Saying, 'What lack you?' and 'Where lies your grief?'
Or 'What good love may I perform for you?'
Many a poor man's son would have lain still
And ne'er have spoke a loving word to you;
But you at your sick service had a prince.
Nay, you may think my love was crafty love,
And call it cunning. Do, an if you will.
If heaven be pleas'd that you must use me ill,
Why then you must. Will you put out mine eyes,
These eyes that never did, nor never shall,
So much as frown on you?

[HUBERT.   I have sworn to do it,
And with hot irons must I burn them out.
PRINCE ARTHUR. Ah, none but in this iron age would do it!]

The iron of itself, though heat red-hot,
Approaching near these eyes, would drink my tears,
And quench his fiery indignation
Even in the matter of mine innocence;
Nay, after that, consume away in rust,
But for containing fire to harm mine eye.
Are you more stubborn-hard than hammer'd iron?
An if an angel should have come to me
And told me Hubert should put out mine eyes,
I would not have believ'd him; no tongue but Hubert's.

   [*Hubert stamps his foot.*
HUBERT. Come forth!
   The Executioners come forth.
                         Do as I bid you do.]

O! Save me, Hubert, save me! My eyes are out
Even with the fierce looks of these bloody men.

[HUBERT (*to Executioners*). Give me the iron, I say, and bind him here.
   He takes the iron.]

Alas, what need you be so boisterous-rough?
I will not struggle, I will stand stone-still.
For heaven's sake, Hubert, let me not be bound!
Nay, hear me, Hubert! Drive these men away,
And I will sit as quiet as a lamb.
I will not stir, nor wince, nor speak a word,
Nor look upon the iron angerly.
Thrust but these men away, and I'll forgive you,
Whatever torment you do put me to. **99**

GLOSSARY

hot irons heated iron pokers
wrought it me embroidered it for me
watchful unsleeping
heavy burdensome
at your sick service while tending to your sickness
crafty devious
an if if
iron age ignoble times
but for containing even for harbouring
what need you be . . . ? why do you have to be . . . ?

King John
William Shakespeare (1596)

WHO ☞ *The Bastard, Philip Faulconbridge, the illegitimate nephew of King John, late teens/20s.*

WHERE ☞ *Amongst the French camp on the field of battle, near St Edmund's-Bury.*

TO WHOM ☞ *Lewis and the rebellious English lords and the French army.*

WHEN ☞ *1201.*

WHAT HAS JUST HAPPENED ☞ *King John's hold on the English throne has been threatened by a rival claimant, his nephew Arthur of Brittany, who is supported by the French King and a number of disloyal English barons. To neutralise the threat, John arranges the marriage of his niece to the heir of the King of France, to whom he also cedes his smaller French possessions. Many of the English subjects abhor this gambit, which they find humiliating, and when the Pope excommunicates John and authorises a French attack on England, the King's strategy falls apart. His army looks set to lose this battle on English soil, though they won the last on French, at Angiers. The Bastard, a calculating social climber with tremendous strength of character, arrives with a flag of truce. He is without a doubt the mainstay of the English force. He has tried before to reunite the English lords with the King's armies and is appealing to Lewis heading the insurgents, to desist, particularly since King John has been recently reunited with Rome. But Lewis's representative refuses. This is the Bastard's response.*

WHAT HE WANTS/OBJECTIVES TO PLAY ☞

- *To brave them out and terrify them.*
- *To belittle them and remind them of England's previous success on French soil.*
- *To admonish the English lords and diminish them as men, as English citizens and as warriors.*

Philip the Bastard

66 By all the blood that ever fury breath'd,
The youth says well. Now hear our English king,
For thus his royalty doth speak in me.
He is prepar'd, and reason too he should:
This apish and unmannerly approach,
This harness'd masque and unadvisèd revel,
This unhair'd sauciness and boyish troops,
The King doth smile at, and is well prepar'd
To whip this dwarfish war, these pigmy arms,
From out the circle of his territories.
That hand which had the strength even at your door
To cudgel you and make you take the hatch,
To dive, like buckets, in concealèd wells,
To crouch in litter of your stable planks,
To lie, like pawns, lock'd up in chests and trunks,
To hug with swine, to seek sweet safety out
In vaults and prisons, and to thrill and shake
Even at the crying of your nation's crow,
Thinking his voice an armèd Englishman;
Shall that victorious hand be feebled here
That in your chambers gave you chastisement?
No! Know the gallant monarch is in arms,
And like an eagle o'er his eyrie towers
To souse annoyance that comes near his nest.
(*To the English lords.*)
And you degenerate, you ingrate revolts,
You bloody Neros, ripping up the womb
Of your dear mother England, blush for shame;
For your own ladies and pale-visag'd maids
Like Amazons come tripping after drums;
Their thimbles into armèd gauntlets change,
Their needles to lances, and their gentle hearts
To fierce and bloody inclination. **99**

GLOSSARY

harness'd masque armoured pageant
unadvis'd revel inappropriate festivity

unhair'd sauciness immature impertinence
take the hatch exit via the lower part of a door
litter animal's bedding
pawns (1) pawned articles; (2) chess pieces
hug with curl up with
souse annoyance swoop down on any danger
ingrate ungrateful
bloody Neros . . . i.e. the Roman Emperor who murdered his mother
Amazons legendary female warriors
tripping dancing

Measure for Measure

William Shakespeare (c.1603)

WHO ☞   *Angelo, deputy to the Duke of Vienna, 30s.*

WHERE ☞   *Duke Vincentio's palace in Vienna.*

TO WHOM ☞ *The audience.*

WHEN ☞   *Contemporary with authorship.*

WHAT HAS JUST HAPPENED ☞ *Empowered by the absentee Duke to reverse the lax morals in Vienna, Angelo imposes the full measure of the law on a young man, Claudio, sentencing him to death for making his fiancée, Juliette, pregnant. Claudio's sister Isabella, a novice nun, has attempted to dissuade Angelo from his harsh judgment. He seems to soften under her influence and asks her to come back the next day to hear his decision. This monologue begins with the soliloquy which occurs after that first meeting, while the second part is spoken just before she comes back the following day, in the following scene, though the two halves work well as one.*

WHAT HE WANTS/OBJECTIVES TO PLAY ☞

- *To ascertain how this attraction, for a nun of all women, could possibly have been engendered.*

- *To question whether this is a perversion in him – she is the most virtuous and unavailable woman possible.*

- *To acknowledge that it is wrong to condemn her brother when he himself is experiencing such strong desire.*

- *To let us know he is in love, though it is a corruptive love, and though it will probably condemn him, he cannot resist it.*

- *To admit his duplicity, aware that his outward show, his words and deeds, contrast sharply with his inner life.*

Angelo

❝ What's this? What's this? Is this her fault, or mine?
The tempter, or the tempted, who sins most, ha?
Not she; nor doth she tempt; but it is I
That, lying by the violet in the sun,
Do as the carrion does, not as the flower,
Corrupt with virtuous season. Can it be
That modesty may more betray our sense
Than woman's lightness? Having waste ground enough,
Shall we desire to raze the sanctuary
And pitch our evils there? O fie, fie, fie!
What dost thou, or what art thou, Angelo?
Dost thou desire her foully for those things
That make her good? O, let her brother live!
Thieves for their robbery have authority,
When judges steal themselves. What, do I love her,
That I desire to hear her speak again,
And feast upon her eyes? What is't I dream on?
O cunning enemy, that, to catch a saint,
With saints doth bait thy hook! Most dangerous
Is that temptation that doth goad us on
To sin in loving virtue. Never could the strumpet
With all her double vigour, art and nature,
Once stir my temper: but this virtuous maid
Subdues me quite. Ever till now
When men were fond, I smil'd, and wonder'd how.

   [*Scene 2.3 omitted here.*]

When I would pray and think, I think and pray
To several subjects: heaven hath my empty words,
Whilst my invention, hearing not my tongue,
Anchors on Isabel; God in my mouth,
As if I did but only chew His name,
And in my heart the strong and swelling evil
Of my conception. The state whereon I studied
Is like a good thing, being often read,
Grown sear'd and tedious. Yea, my gravity,

Wherein – let no man hear me – I take pride,
Could I with boot change for an idle plume
Which the air beats in vain. O place, O form,
How often dost thou with thy case, thy habit,
Wrench awe from fools, and tie the wiser souls
To thy false seeming! Blood, thou art blood.
Let's write 'good angel' on the devil's horn –
'Tis now the devil's crest. **99**

GLOSSARY

carrion putrefying flesh
virtuous season growing time of the year
pitch (1) set up; (2) cast away
fond lovesick
sear'd dried up
boot advantage
idle plume frivolous feather (worn in the hat)
form ceremony, status
case clothing, garb
habit vestment
crest heraldic emblem

The Widow's Tears

George Chapman (1604)

WHO ☞   *Lysander, 20s plus.*

WHERE ☞   *On a street.*

TO WHOM ☞   *Himself (his brother has just left).*

WHEN ☞   *Contemporary with authorship.*

WHAT HAS JUST HAPPENED ☞   *In this comedy Tharsalio tries to convince his brother, Lysander, that all women are prone to cheating on their husbands and taking lovers soon into their widowhood. Tharsalio has set his sights on Eudora, the widow countess, and plans to prove his bet to Lysander by wooing her into bed. Meanwhile, Lysander has overheard his brother speaking about an infidelity by Tharsalio's own wife, Cynthia, and begs him to tell all. Tharsalio insists that curiosity can be the undoing of a happy marriage, and refuses to tell him this secret wrongdoing. Just prior to this soliloquy, Lysander tries again to confront his brother, to no avail. His brother knows how to wind Lysander up, and has just done so, beautifully.*

WHAT HE WANTS/OBJECTIVES TO PLAY ☞

- *To vent his frustration, rage and agony over the latent accusations of his wife's fidelity.*

- *To convince himself – and the audience – that his brother is a lout and his opinion worthless because of the sort of man he is.*

- *To make himself feel better about the accusation, to calm himself down.*

- *To defend his wife's honour, and save himself from the title of 'cuckold'.*

Lysander

" All the Furies in hell attend thee; 'Has given me a bone to
tire on with a pestilence. 'Slight, know?
What can he know? What can his eye observe
More than mine own, or the most piercing sight
That ever view'd her? By this light, I think
Her privat'st thought may dare the eye of heaven,
And challenge th'envious world to witness it.
I know him for a wild, corrupted youth,
Whom profane ruffians, squires to bawds and strumpets,
Drunkards spew'd out of taverns into th'sinks
Of tap-houses and stews, revolts from manhood,
Debauch'd perdus, have by their companies
Turn'd devil like themselves, and stuff'd his soul
With damn'd opinions and unhallow'd thoughts
Of womanhood, of all humanity,
Nay, deity itself. **"**

GLOSSARY

tire on feed ravenously on
with a pestilence furiously, 'with a vengeance'
'slight by God's light!
profane irreverent
stews brothels
revolts degenerates
debauch'd perdus corrupt desperados
unhallow'd wicked

The Honest Whore

Thomas Dekker (1604)

WHO ☞ *Hippolyto, a gentleman beloved of Infelice, the daughter of The Duke of Milan.*

WHERE ☞ *In Bellafront's lodging, Milan.*

TO WHOM ☞ *Bellafront, a whore who has declared her undying love for him.*

WHEN ☞ *Contemporary with authorship.*

WHAT HAS JUST HAPPENED ☞ *Hippolyto has been convinced by the Duke of Milan that Infelice has died, as he has convinced her that Hippolyto has died, such is his disapproval of their love for each other and yearning to marry each other. Hippolyto vows to his friend, Matheo, that he shall stay faithful to the memory of his love. They have arrived at the house of a prostitute, Bellafront, who has previously lost her virtue to Matheo. She is immediately taken with Hippolyto. But he rejects her advances and is highly critical of her immorality. This is the speech that prompts the moral conversion of the prostitute to the honest whore of the title. It might be useful to remember that she is the opposite of Infelice, and all the rage – and sexual frustration – which he carries for not being able to be with her, can be fuelled into this speech.*

WHAT HE WANTS / OBJECTIVES TO PLAY ☞

- *To diminish her as just one of her profession.*
- *To dismiss out of hand her honourable love for him.*
- *To insult her.*
- *To let her know that he believes all her life is about extortion, all about money.*
- *To warn her that she has a lonely, impoverished and miserable death ahead of her, as befits all 'her kind'.*
- *To leave her in no doubt that he is repulsed by her and what she represents.*

Hippolyto

" Lend me your silence and attention.
You have no soul; that makes you weigh so light:
Heaven's treasure bought it
And half a crown hath sold it, for your body
Is like the common shore that still receives
All the town's filth. The sin of many men
Is within you, and thus much I suppose,
That if all your committers stood in rank,
They'd make a lane in which your shame might dwell,
And with their spaces reach from hence to hell.
Nay, shall I urge it more? There has been known
As many by one harlot, maim'd and dismember'd,
As would ha' stuff'd an hospital: this I might
Apply to you, and perhaps do you right.
Oh, y'are as base as any beast that bears:
Your body is e'en hir'd, and so are theirs!
For gold and sparkling jewels, if he can,
You'll let a Jew get you with Christian,
Be he a Moor, a Tartar, tho' his face
Look uglier than a dead man's skull;
Could the devil put on a human shape,
If his purse shake out crowns, up then he gets.
Whores will be rid to hell with golden bits:
So that you're crueller than Turks, for they
Sell Christians only, you sell yourselves away.
Why, those that love you, hate you, and will term you
Lickerish damnation, wish themselves half sunk
After the sin is laid out, and e'en curse
Their fruitless riot, for what one begets
Another poisons. Lust and murder hit.
A tree being often shook, what fruit can knit? [. . .]

Methinks a toad is happier than a whore,
That with one poison, swells; with thousands more
The other stocks her veins. Harlot? Fie, fie!
You are the miserablest creatures breathing,
The very slaves of nature. Mark me else.

You put on rich attires: others' eyes wear them;
You eat but to supply your blood with sin.
And this strange curse e'en haunts you to your graves:
From fools you get, and spend it upon slaves.
Like bears and apes, you're baited and show tricks
For money, but your bawd the sweetness licks.
Indeed, you are their journeywomen, and do
All base and damn'd works they list set you to,
So that you ne'er are rich; for do but show me,
In present memory or in ages past,
The fairest and most famous courtesan,
Whose flesh was dear'st; that rais'd the price of sin,
And held it up; to whose intemperate bosom,
Princes, earls, lords (the worst has been a knight,
The mean'st a gentleman), have offer'd up
Whole hecatombs of sighs, and rain'd in showers
Handfuls of gold; yet, for all this, at last
Diseases suck'd her marrow, then grew so poor
That she has begg'd, e'en at a beggar's door.
And (wherein heaven has a finger) when this idol,
From coast to coast, has leap'd on foreign shores,
And had more worship than th' outlandish whores;
When several nations have gone over her;
When, for each several city she has seen,
Her maidenhead has been new, and been sold dear;
Did live well there, and might have died unknown
And undefam'd – back comes she to her own,
And there both miserably lives and dies,
Scorn'd even of those that once ador'd her eyes,
As if her fatal, circled life thus ran:
Her pride should end there where it first began.
What, do you weep to hear your story read?

[BELLAFONT. Oh yes, I pray proceed:
Indeed, 'twill do me good to weep, indeed.]

To give those tears a relish, this I add:
You're like the Jews, scatter'd, in no place certain;
Your days are tedious, your hours burdensome;
And were't not for full suppers, midnight revels,

Dancing, wine, riotous meetings, which do drown
And bury quite in you all virtuous thoughts,
And on your eyelids hang so heavily,
They have no power to look so high as heaven,
You'd sit and muse on nothing but despair.
Curse that devil lust that so burns up your blood
And in ten thousand shivers break your glass
For his temptation! Say you taste delight,
To have a golden gull from rise to set,
To meet you in his hot luxurious arms,
Yet your nights pay for all: I know you dream
Of warrants, whips, and beadles, and then start
At a door's windy creak, think every weasel
To be a constable, and every rat
A long-tail'd officer. Are you now not slaves?
Oh, you have damnation without pleasure for it!
Such is the state of harlots. To conclude,
When you are old and can well paint no more,
You turn bawd, and are then worse than before.
Make use of this; farewell. **99**

GLOSSARY

beasts that bear beasts of burden
lickerish lustful
bits components of a horse's bridle
hit be in accord
knit generate
hecatombs
list wish to
[*shivers* splinters
golden gull rich client
beadles parish constables

The Dutch Courtesan

John Marston (1604)

WHO ☞   *Malheureux, French for 'unhappy', Freevill's friend, early 20s.*

WHERE ☞   *In a brothel, London.*

TO WHOM ☞   *The audience.*

WHEN ☞   *Contemporary with authorship.*

WHAT HAS JUST HAPPENED ☞   *Freevill is deeply involved with Franceschina, the 'Dutch Courtesan' of the title, but he is set to marry the virtuous Beatrice and has to end his relationship with Franceschina. He is terrified of how she will react and so in a rather cowardly way, introduces her to a friend of his, Malheureux, in an attempt to palm her off. It works: Malheureux is bowled over by her. However, when Franceschina finds out Freevill's plan, she is humiliated and furious. She has just attempted to persuade Malheureux to kill Freevill and bring her the ring that Beatrice gave him as a token, in return for her love.*

WHAT HE WANTS/OBJECTIVES TO PLAY ☞

- *To express horror at what is asked of him.*

- *To reason with his higher self that he might do the honourable thing.*

- *To battle against his baser instincts which are to give in to his carnal desires.*

Malheureux

❝ To kill my friend! O 'tis to kill myself!
Yet man's but man's excrement, man breeding man
As he does worms, or this. (*He spits.*) To spoil this, nothing!
The body of a man is of the selfsame soil
As ox or horse; no murder to kill these.
As for that only part which makes us man,
Murder wants power to touch't. – O wit, how vile,
How hellish art thou when thou raisest nature
'Gainst sacred faith! Think more – to kill a friend
To gain a woman, to lose a virtuous self
For appetite and sensual end, whose very having
Loseth all appetite and gives satiety,
That corporal end, remorse and inward blushings
Forcing us loathe the steam of our own heats,
Whilst friendship clos'd in virtue, being spiritual,
Tastes no such languishings and moment's pleasure
With much repentance, but like rivers flow,
And further that they run, they bigger grow.
Lord, how was I misgone! How easy 'tis to err
When passion will not give us leave to think!
A learn'd that is an honest man may fear,
And lust, and rage, and malice, and anything
When he is taken uncollected suddenly:
'Tis sin of cold blood, mischief with wak'd eyes,
That is the damnèd and the truly vice,
Not he that's passionless, but he 'bove passion's wise.
My friend shall know it all. **❞**

GLOSSARY

misgone gone astray

A Mad World, My Masters

Thomas Middleton (1605)

WHO ☞ *Discharged soldier Captain Dick Follywit, an impoverished gallant. His name means 'foolish intelligence' or 'stupid senses'. 20s/30s.*

WHERE ☞ *On the London streets.*

TO WHOM ☞ *Lieutenant Mawworm, Ancient Hoboy and other comrades and consorts, all 'true and necessary implements of mischief'.*

WHEN ☞ *Spring 1605.*

WHAT HAS JUST HAPPENED ☞ *In this opening scene, we are introduced to Dick and his merry gang of charismatic ne'er-do-wells. While there is good-natured banter between them, the fact is they are hungry and they have no money. In this speech Dick, asserting his position as their leader, reveals a plan. Set to inherit a fortune from his grandfather, Sir Bounteous Progress, Dick's logic is that he may as well get it early by disguising himself as a lord and tricking Sir Bounteous, rather than wait until the man dies.*

WHAT HE WANTS/OBJECTIVES TO PLAY ☞

- *To inspire them with his plan out of misery and hunger.*
- *To cheer them.*
- *To get them on side with his plan.*
- *To vent his spleen about that generation who will give nothing when living but bequeath all when dead.*
- *To reinstate their faith in him as their leader.*

Richard Follywit

❝ Nay, faith, as for blushing, I think there's grace little enough amongst you all: 'tis Lent in your cheeks, the flag's down. Well, your blushing face I suspect not, nor indeed greatly your laughing face, unless you had more money in your purses. Then, thus, compendiously, now. You all know the possibilities of my hereafter-fortunes, and the humour of my frolic grandsire Sir Bounteous Progress, whose death makes all possible to me: I shall have all, when he has nothing – but now he has all, I shall have nothing.
I think one mind runs through a million of 'em: they love to keep us sober all the while they're alive, that when they're dead we may drink to their healths; they cannot abide to see us merry all the while they're above ground, and that makes so many laugh at their fathers' funerals. I know my grandsire has his will in a box, and has bequeathed all to me when he can carry nothing away: but stood I in need of poor ten pounds now, by his will I should hang myself ere I should get it. There's no such word in his will, I warrant you, nor no such thought in his mind.

[MAWWORM. You may build upon that, Captain.]

Then, since he has no will to do me good as he lives, by mine own will I'll do myself good before he dies; And now I arrive at the purpose. You are not ignorant, I'm sure (you true and necessary implements of mischief), first, that my grandsire Sir Bounteous Progress is a knight of thousands (and therefore no knight, since one thousand six hundred); next, that he keeps a house like his name, bounteous, open for all comers; thirdly and lastly, that he stands much upon the glory of his complement, variety of entertainment, together with the largeness of his kitchen, longitude of his buttery, and fecundity of his larder, and thinks himself never happier than when some stiff lord or great countess alights, to make light his dishes. These being well mixed together may give my project better encouragement, and make my purpose spring forth more fortunate. To be short (and cut off a great deal of dirty way) I'll down to my grandsire like a lord.

[MAWWORM. How, Captain?]

A French ruff, a thin beard, and a strong perfume will do't. I can hire blue coats for you all by Westminster clock, and that colour will be soonest believed. **99**

GLOSSARY

the flag's down a reference to the flags flown by theatres during performances; plays were forbidden during Lent.
compendiously comprehensively, in summary
frolic merry
of thousands worth thousands
one thousand six hundred a reference to the 'hundred-pound knights' who bought their honours from King James for cash on his accession in 1603.
complement hospitality
buttery wine cellar
blue coats servants' livery

A Mad World, My Masters

Thomas Middleton (1605)

WHO ☞ *Master Penitent Brothel. 'An admirer of Mistress Harebrain', the wife of his friend. 20s plus.*

WHERE ☞ *The Harebrains' home, evening.*

TO WHOM ☞ *Mistress Harebrain.*

WHEN ☞ *Contemporary with authorship.*

WHAT HAS JUST HAPPENED ☞ *Penitent has been lusting after his friend Harebrain's wife for a long time. Having hatched a plan to disguise himself as a doctor so he might see her alone, he suffers terrible pangs of conscience. That evening he is visited by a devilish spirit – in the physical form of Mistress Harebrain, a 'succubus' who terrifies him with taunting and libidinous insinuation. Assuming this must have been the Mistress in disguise, maybe to scare him, he rushes to her home where she assures him not only that it wasn't her, but she does not even know where he lives, has not left home all evening and she must now be damned! He wants nothing more to do with this possible affair; he has been terrified out of his wits.*

WHAT HE WANTS/OBJECTIVES TO PLAY ☞

- *To release her and himself from this devilish bond of adulterous love.*

- *To leave her in no doubt as to the gravity of what they have almost given in to – through her enticement and his lust.*

- *To urge her to be a good wife and remain faithful, always, to her husband.*

- *Where indicated, her husband joins him: at this point Penitent wants to bless them as a perfect and loving couple, formalising their union and thereby excluding himself totally from it.*

Penitent Brothel

❝ Burst into sorrow then, and grief's extremes,
Whilst I beat on this flesh!

[WIFE. What is't disturbs you, sir?
PENITENT. Then was the devil in your likeness there.
WIFE. Ha?]

The very devil assum'd thee formally:
That face, that voice, that gesture, that attire,
E'en as it sits on thee, not a pleat alter'd,
That beaver-band, the colour of that periwig,
The farthingale above the navel, all,
As if the fashion were his own invention.

[WIFE. Mercy defend me!]

                              To beguile me more,
The cunning succubus told me that meeting
Was wrought o' purpose by much wit and art,
Wept to me, laid my vows before me, urg'd me,
Gave me the private marks of all our love,
Woo'd me in wanton and effeminate rhymes,
And sung and danc'd about me like a fairy,
And had not worthier cogitations bless'd me,
Thy form and his enchantments had possess'd me.

[WIFE. What shall become of me? My own thoughts doom me.]

Be honest: then the devil will ne'er assume thee.
He has no pleasure in that shape to abide,
Where these two sisters reign not, Lust or Pride.
He as much trembles at a constant mind
As looser flesh at him. – Be not dismay'd:
Spring souls for joy, his policies are betray'd.
Forgive me, Mistress Harebrain, on whose soul
The guilt hangs double,
My lust and thy enticement: both I challenge,
And therefore of due vengeance it appear'd
To none but me, to whom both sins inher'd.
What knows the lecher when he clips his whore

Whether it be the devil his parts adore?
They're both so like, that in our natural sense,
I could discern no change nor difference.
No marvel then times should so stretch and turn:
None for religion, all for pleasure burn.
Hot zeal into hot lust is now transform'd,
Grace into painting, charity into clothes,
Faith into false hair – and put off as often.
There's nothing but our virtue knows a mean:
He that kept open house now keeps a quean,
He will keep open still, that he commends,
And there he keeps a table for his friends;
And she consumes more than his sire could hoard,
Being more common than his house or board.

Enter Harebrain

Live honest, and live happy, keep thy vows,
She's part a virgin whom but one man knows.
Embrace thy husband, and beside him none,
Having but one heart, give it but to one. 99

GLOSSARY

beaver-band a hat's fur trimming
farthingale long, hooped dress
succubus devilish woman
effeminate tender
cogitations ruminations, trains of thought
clips embraces
painting i.e. make-up
There's nothing but our virtue knows a mean Only virtue can moderate
    our behaviour
quean whore

Volpone

Ben Jonson (1606)

WHO ☞   *Corvino, a merchant, 30s plus.*

WHERE ☞   *In Corvino's house.*

TO WHOM ☞   *Celia, his wife.*

WHEN ☞   *Contemporary with authorship.*

WHAT HAS JUST HAPPENED ☞   *Corvino does not know that Volpone, of the title, has been wooing Celia at her window, incognito, and that he is smitten by her. Corvino is impossibly jealous and paranoid in even normal circumstances, but here he is incandescent with rage, having just dragged her from the window where he believes she has made a fool of herself by communing with this suitor with the town's elderly men looking on, making a fool of him too.*

WHAT HE WANTS/OBJECTIVES TO PLAY ☞

- *To put the fear of God into her.*

- *To let her know that the repercussions of her appalling behaviour – the introduction of an even more stringent control – are her own fault.*

- *To refuse her protestation of innocence point blank.*

- *To ridicule and taunt her with condemnation of her sexually suggestive conduct to the point where she will have no will or opinion of her own whatsoever.*

- *To immobilise her with moral instruction and in so doing regain his own lost dignity.*

Corvino

❝ Death of mine honour, with the city's fool?
A juggling, tooth-drawing, prating mountebank?
And at a public window? Where, whilst he

With his strain'd action and his dole of faces
To his drug-lecture draws your itching ears,
A crew of old, unmarried, noted lechers
Stood leering up like satyrs? And you smile
Most graciously, and fan your favours forth,
To give your hot spectators satisfaction!
What, was your mountebank their call? Their whistle?
Or were you enamour'd on his copper rings,
His saffron jewel with the toad-stone in't,
Or his embroider'd suit with the cope-stitch,
Made of a hearse cloth? Or his old tilt-feather?
Or his starch'd beard? Well, you shall have him, yes!
He shall come home and minister unto you
The fricace for the mother. Or, let me see,
I think you'd rather mount? Would you not mount?
Why, if you'll mount, you may; yes truly, you may –
And so you may be seen down to th' foot.
Get you a cittern, Lady Vanity,
And be a dealer with the Virtuous Man;
Make one. I'll but protest myself a cuckold,
And save your dowry. [. . .]

And thy restraint before was liberty
To what I now decree; and therefore mark me.
First, I will have this bawdy light damm'd up;
And till't be done, some two, or three yards off
I'll chalk a line, o'er which if thou but chance
To set thy desp'rate foot, more hell, more horror,
More wild, remorseless rage shall seize on thee
Than on a conjuror that had heedless left
His circle's safety ere his devil was laid.
Then, here's a lock, which I will hang upon thee;
And, now I think on't, I will keep thee backwards;
Thy lodging shall be backwards, thy walks backwards;
Thy prospect – all be backwards, and no pleasure,
That thou shalt know but backwards. Nay, since you force
My honest nature, know it is your own
Being too open makes me use you thus.
Since you will not contain your subtle nostrils

In a sweet room, but they must snuff the air
Of rank and sweaty passengers –

Knock within.

One knocks.
Away, and be not seen, pain of thy life;
Nor look toward the window; if thou dost –
Nay, stay, hear this – let me not prosper, whore,
But I will make thee an anatomy,
Dissect thee mine own self, and read a lecture
Upon thee to the city, and in public.
Away! 〞

GLOSSARY

mountebank one who deceives others
juggling cheating
strain'd action exaggerated performance
dole of faces stock of facial expressions
drug-lecture mountebank's sales-patter
satyrs mythological man-goats
hot lustful
toad-stone precious stone, a supposed elixir
hearse cloth elaborate drapery for coffins at funerals
copper rings cheap substitutes for gold
cope-stitch resembling a cloak
tilt-feather ostrich plume from a jousting helmet
starch'd fashionably stiffened
fricace for the mother massage for hysteria
mount (1) get up on stage; (2) copulate
cittern stringed instrument (associated with vice)
Lady Vanity . . . Virtuous Man characters of an imagined morality play
make one (1) make up one of their number; (2) perform a sexual act
Save your dowry if a wife was unfaithful her dowry reverted to her
    husband
Dutchman one of a complacent nature
entertain a parley conduct a conversation
light window
conjuror magician
laid exorcised
lock chastity belt
backwards facing the back of the house
make thee an anatomy analyse your moral qualities

The Revenger's Tragedy

Cyril Tourneur? (1607)

WHO ☞ *Vindice. His name means 'revenger of wrongs'. 20s/30s.*

WHERE ☞ *The Duke's premises in an Italian Court.*

TO WHOM ☞ *The audience.*

WHEN ☞ *Contemporary with the authorship.*

WHAT HAS JUST HAPPENED ☞ *This is the opening speech of the play. The stage direction reads, 'Enter Vindice holding a skull; he watches the Duke, Duchess, Lussurioso his son, Spurio, the bastard, with a train, pass over the stage with torch-light'. Nine years ago Vindice lost his love when the Duke, after she resisted his advances, poisoned her. Having recently lost his father through the Duke's unkindness, Vindice wants revenge.*

WHAT HE WANTS/OBJECTIVES TO PLAY ☞

• *To conjure the world of this play in his descriptions of the 'Four excellent characters' as they pass. Rather than commenting on their morality, Vindice's aim is to reduce them to mere types – the ageing adulterer, the lecherous heir, the calculating step-mother, and the bastard, who, as a bastard, the original audience would expect to behave in nothing less than a despicable fashion.*

• *To let the audience in on the extent of his loathing for the Duke and his desperate need for revenge.*

• *To communicate his great love for the woman whose skull he holds.*

Vindice

" Duke; royal lecher; go, grey-hair'd Adultery;
And thou his son, as impious steep'd as he;
And thou his bastard, true-begot in evil;
And thou his duchess, that will do with devil.
Four excellent characters – O, that marrowless age
Would stuff the hollow bones with damn'd desires,
And 'stead of heat, kindle infernal fires
Within the spendthrift veins of a dry duke,
A parch'd and juiceless luxur. O God! – one
That has scarce blood enough to live upon,
And he to riot it like a son and heir?
O, the thought of that
Turns my abusèd heart-strings into fret.
Thou sallow picture of my poison'd love,
My study's ornament, thou shell of Death,
Once the bright face of my betrothèd lady,
When life and beauty naturally fill'd out
These ragged imperfections,
When two heaven-pointed diamonds were set
In those unsightly rings – then 'twas a face
So far beyond the artificial shine
Of any woman's bought complexion,
That the uprightest man (if such there be
That sin but seven times a day) broke custom,
And made up eight with looking after her.
O, she was able to ha' made a usurer's son
Melt all his patrimony in a kiss,
And what his father fifty years told,
To have consum'd, and yet his suit been cold.
But O, accursèd palace!
Thee when thou wert apparell'd in thy flesh
The old duke poison'd,
Because thy purer part would not consent
Unto his palsy-lust; for old men lustful
Do show like young men, angry, eager, violent,
Outbid like their limited performances.

O 'ware an old man hot and vicious:
Age, as in gold, in lust is covetous.
Vengeance, thou Murder's quit-rent, and whereby
Thou show'st thyself tenant to Tragedy,
O, keep thy day, hour, minute, I beseech,
For those thou hast determin'd! – hum, who e'er knew
Murder unpaid? Faith, give Revenge her due,
She's kept touch hitherto – be merry, merry,
Advance thee, O thou terror to fat folks,
To have their costly three-pil'd flesh worn off
As bare as this – for banquets, ease and laughter,
Can make great men, as greatness goes by clay;
But wise men, little, are more great than they. **99**

GLOSSARY

do with copulate with
luxur lecher
turn my abusèd heart-strings into fret untune the strings of my damaged
    heart into discordant anger
told accrued, counted up
palsy-lust senile lechery
'ware beware of
quit-rent the standing charge paid by a tenant to his landlord
determin'd settled on
three-pil'd three-layered
by clay in terms of the flesh only

The Tamer Tamed

John Fletcher (1611)

WHO ☞   *Petruchio, the character first met in* The
Taming of the Shrew. *He is best known as a wife tamer. 30s
plus.*

WHERE ☞   *Outside Petruchio's house in Italy.*

TO WHOM ☞   *The audience.*

WHEN ☞   *Contemporary with the authorship.*

WHAT HAS JUST HAPPENED ☞   *Kate, Petruchio's wife, has
died; he has recently re-married her cousin Maria, who is more
than a match for him. She has been defying her new husband's
every demand – including shunning the marital 'duties' in the
bedroom. She wants to break him, just as Petruchio believes he
broke her cousin Kate. Petruchio has been feigning illness in an
attempt to win his wife's pity – it has backfired, she has caught
on to his ruse and is playing along with it, only boosting the story
somewhat in her own inimitable way. She has told everyone he
has the plague, it is contagious, no one is to go into the house; she
has locked him in and she has advised him and all that know him
that he has only days to live. The watchmen who were set outside
the house to stop him coming out or anyone going in, have just
run off as Petruchio's desperate vitriol has terrified them as he
breaks down the door, livid and armed with a gun!*

WHAT HE WANTS/OBJECTIVES TO PLAY ☞

- *To warn every man in the audience of the duplicity of all
  wives – however seemingly 'nice'.*

- *To impress upon the audience that if any male member is not
  already married, then he must never take the risk and get
  married.*

- *To educate men who may not know how wives systematically
  destroy their husbands.*

Petruchio

66 The door shall open too, I'll have a fair shoot.

Petruchio bursts the door open and enters with a gun.

Are ye all gone? Tricks in my old days, crackers
Put now upon me? And by Lady Greensleeves?
When a man has the fairest and the sweetest
Of all their sex, and, as he think the noblest,
What has he then? I'll speak modestly:
He has a quartern-ague that shall shake
All his estate to nothing: out on 'em, hedgehogs!
He that shall touch 'em has a thousand thorns
Run through his fingers. If I were unmarried,
I would do anything below repentance,
Any base dunghill slavery, be a hangman,
Ere I would be a husband. O, the thousand,
Thousand, ten thousand ways they have to kill us!
Some fall with too much stringing of the fiddles,
And those are fools: some that they are not suffer'd,
And those are maudlin lovers: some, like scorpions,
They poison with their tails, and those are martyrs;
Some die with doing good, those benefactors,
And leave 'em land to leap away; some few,
For those are rarest, they are said to kill
With kindness and fair usage, but what they are
My catalogue discovers not, only 'tis thought
They are buried in old walls with their heels upward.
I could rail twenty days together now.
I'll seek 'em out, and if I have not reason,
And very sensible, why this was done,
I'll go a-birding yet, and some shall smart for't. **99**

GLOSSARY

Lady Greensleeves the beloved object of the song 'Greensleeves'
quartern ague chronic feaver
stringing of the fiddles sex
suffer'd allowed
leap away fritter away
smart feel pain

The Duchess of Malfi

John Webster (1613)

WHO ☞ *Ferdinand, the Duke of Calabria and brother to the Duchess of the title. 20s plus.*

WHERE ☞ *A prison near the Shrine of Loretto, Italy.*

TO WHOM ☞ *Bosola, a spy, referring to the corpse of his murdered sister the Duchess – murdered at his command.*

WHEN ☞ *Contemporary with authorship.*

WHAT HAS JUST HAPPENED ☞ *Ferdinand and his brother, the Cardinal, forbade their widowed sister, the Duchess, to remarry. This was for reasons of financial gain on their part. But after falling in love with the honourable Antonio, she disobeyed them, marrying in secret and bearing but low-born Antonio three children, again without anyone knowing. The Duchess believed Bosola to be a trusted member of her household; not knowing he was in the pay of her brothers, spying on her and her family, she let her guard slip. Once the brothers found out, Antonio and the eldest child fled north, under the pretence that the Duchess had exiled him, her plan being to reunite the family later, at a safer time. However Bosola engineered the butchering of the Duchess's children and on Ferdinand's orders, has strangled her, and all for a princely sum. Ferdinand has just joined Bosola with the corpse and at the sight of his dead twin, is filled with a sort of remorse for himself and loathing for Bosola for carrying out his orders.*

WHAT HE WANTS/OBJECTIVES TO PLAY ☞

- *To absolve himself of any blame, he is re-writing history to suit himself by saying he was out of his mind when issuing the order and Bosola should have recognised this.*

- *To blame Bosola entirely for the murders.*

- *To cover himself, should the deaths ever be linked back to him: he was not responsible!*

- *To make himself feel better about the appalling deed engineered by him and his brother.*

Ferdinand

" Cover her face. Mine eyes dazzle: she died young.

[BOSOLA. I think not so: her infelicity
Seem'd to have years too many.]

She and I were twins:
And should I die this instant, I had liv'd
Her time to a minute.

[BOSOLA.   It seems she was born first.
You have bloodily approv'd the ancient truth,
That kindred commonly do worse agree
Than remote strangers.]

                        Let me see her face again;
Why didst not thou pity her? What an excellent
Honest man mightst thou have been
If thou hadst borne her to some sanctuary!
Or, bold in a good cause, oppos'd thyself
With thy advancèd sword above thy head,
Between her innocence and my revenge!
I bade thee, when I was distracted of my wits,
Go kill my dearest friend, and thou hast done't.
For let me but examine well the cause:
What was the meanness of her match to me?
Only I must confess, I had a hope,
Had she continued widow, to have gain'd
An infinite mass of treasure by her death:
And that was the main cause; her marriage,
That drew a stream of gall quite through my heart;
For thee (as we observe in tragedies
That a good actor many times is curs'd
For playing a villain's part), I hate thee for't:
And, for my sake say thou hast done much ill, well.

[BOSOLA. Let me quicken your memory: for I perceive
You are falling into ingratitude. I challenge
The reward due to my service.
FERDINAND.   I'll tell thee
What I'll give thee –

BOSOLA.   Do.
FERDINAND.   I'll give thee a pardon
For this murder.
BOSOLA.   Ha?
FERDINAND.   Yes: and 'tis
The largest bounty I can study to do thee.]

By what authority didst thou execute
This bloody sentence?

[BOSOLA.   By yours]

                    Mine? Was I her judge?
Did any ceremonial form of law
Doom her to not-being? Did a complete jury
Deliver her conviction up i'th'court?
Where shalt thou find this judgement register'd
Unless in hell? See: like a bloody fool
Th'hast forfeited thy life, and thou shalt die for't. **99**

GLOSSARY

infelicity misfortune
meanness of the match lowliness of her marriage
gall bitterness
quicken refresh
challen ge claim

A Chaste Maid in Cheapside

Thomas Middleton (1613)

WHO ☞ *Mr John Allwit, late 20s plus. A man 'kept' by Sir Walter Whorehound together with his wife and family.*

WHERE ☞ *A street off Cheapside, the main marketplace of London.*

TO WHOM ☞ *The audience.*

WHEN ☞ *Contemporary with authorship.*

WHAT HAS JUST HAPPENED ☞ *This soliloquy, spoken by Mr Allwit, conjures the world of this London comedy set during Lent, a world that revolves around illicit sex, debauchery and duplicity. He is a complacent and complicit cuckold, and he and his wife's seven children (fathered by the lover) and servants live off their 'benefactor' Sir Walter. The Allwits are a commercial enterprise rather than a married couple. And Allwit has just heard that Sir Walter is back in town. He is over the moon!*

WHAT HE WANTS/OBJECTIVES TO PLAY ☞

- *To let the audience 'know the score': that he is a married man, not only condoning the 'founder's' relationship with his wife but rejoicing in it.*

- *To introduce the audience to the morality and the language of this world.*

- *To impress the listeners with his philosophy, and maybe to educate them too!*

- *To mock Sir Walter, for being such a fool that he both pays for the keep of another man's wife and family, but also wastes his energy being jealous over a woman he is not even married to.*

John Allwit

" The founder's come to town; I am like a man
Finding a table furnish'd to his hand,
As mine is still to me, prays for the founder;
Bless the right worshipful, the good founder's life.
I thank him; h'as maintain'd my house this ten years,
Not only keeps my wife, but a keeps me,
And all my family; I am at his table,
He gets me all my children, and pays the nurse,
Monthly, or weekly, puts me to nothing,
Rent, nor church duties, not so much as the scavenger:
The happiest state that ever man was born to.
I walk out in a morning, come to breakfast,
Find excellent cheer, a good fire in winter,
Look in my coal house about Midsummer Eve,
That's full, five or six chaldron, new laid up;
Look in my back yard, I shall find a steeple
Made up with Kentish faggots, which o'erlooks
The waterhouse and the windmills; I say nothing
But smile, and pin the door. When she lies in,
As now she's even upon the point of grunting,
A lady lies not in like her; there's her embossings,
Embroiderings, spanglings, and I know not what,
As if she lay with all the gaudy shops
In Gresham's Burse about her; then her restoratives,
Able to set up a young 'pothecary,
And richly stock the foreman of a drug shop;
Her sugar by whole loaves, her wines by rundlets.
I see these things, but like a happy man,
I pay for none at all, yet fools think's mine;
I have the name, and in his gold I shine.
And where some merchants would in soul kiss hell
To buy a paradise for their wives, and dye
Their conscience in the bloods of prodigal heirs
To deck their night-piece, yet all this being done
Eaten with jealousy to the inmost bone –
As what affliction nature more constrains,

Than feed the wife plump for another's veins? –
These torments stand I freed of, I am as clear
From jealousy of a wife as from the charge.
O two miraculous blessings; 'tis the knight
Hath took that labour all out of my hands;
I may sit still and play; he's jealous for me –
Watches her steps, sets spies – I live at ease;
He has both the cost and torment; when the strings
Of his heart frets, I feed, laugh, or sing,
La dildo, dildo la dildo, la dildo dildo de dildo. **99**

GLOSSARY

a he
scavenger lowly civic officer
chaldron a measure of weight
faggots firewood
upon the point of grunting about to give birth
the waterhouse and the windmills a building in a desirable location, on
    the Thames.
embossings . . . spanglings crafted leatherwork . . .decorated fabric
Gresham's Burse The Royal Exchange (built by Thomas Gresham in
    1568)
restoratives medicines
'pothecary apothecary; chemist
rundlets barrels
think's think it is
night-piece bedfellow
La dildo . . . dildo a nonsense ditty (*dildo* = phallic sex-toy)

The Custom of the Country

John Fletcher and Philip Massinger (c. 1619)

WHO ☞   *Duarte, 20s, a braggart gentleman. Nephew of the Governor of Lisbon.*

WHERE ☞   *In the Governor's quarters, Lisbon.*

TO WHOM ☞   *His Page. Though his mother, Guiomar, and uncle, Manuel, are listening in, unseen. He is talking about Don Alonso.*

WHEN ☞   *Contemporary with authorship.*

WHAT HAS JUST HAPPENED ☞ *We have just heard an exchange between his mother and uncle, which sets Duarte's character up in the play, this being the first time we meet him; they despair of his behaviour. He wasn't always a boastful and arrogant liability – he has become one. He is 'out of control'. Evidenced by this latest challenge to a great sea captain. Duarte is increasingly going about insulting just about anyone and spoiling for a fight, generally on totally arbitrary grounds, as in this instance – even very powerful men, and men who are much stronger than him. Those he challenges are compromised in retaliation somewhat because of his powerful relative.*

The Page has just told Duarte that Don Alonso, the great sea captain's nephew, the same sea captain Duarte is trying to pick a fight with, has been making a disparaging comparison between himself and Duarte in public – saying he, Alonso, is the superior man; and to further fan the flames of Duarte's arrogance, Alonso's uncle won't rise to the bait offered, but is rather ignoring it.

WHAT HE WANTS/OBJECTIVES TO PLAY ☞

- *To let the Page, and the world, know that he has gained his reputation in spite of the fact that he is related to the Governor, not because he is – unlike Don Alonso.*

- *To restate that he has earned his standing in society through sheer force of character, intellect and natural authority.*

- *To really enjoy his fantasy of himself as a noble warrior; he is almost overwhelmed, so moved is he by his own descriptions of himself in another life.*

- *To wield his intellect like a rhetorical axe – he is well educated and enjoys revealing that.*

- *To impress the Page – he can't help himself, his instinct is always to make a huge impression on whomsoever he is speaking to, even a servant – and let him know that he is not in the least bit bothered by this affair.*

Duarte

" I look down upon him
With such contempt and scorn as on my slave.
He's a name only, and all good in him
He must derive from his great grandsire's ashes;
For had not their victorious acts bequeath'd
His titles to him and wrote on his forehead,
'This is a Lord', he had liv'd unobserv'd
By any man of mark, and died as one
Among the common rout. Compare with me?
'Tis giant-like ambition. I know him
And know myself. That man is truly noble,
And he may justly call that worth his own,
Which his deserts have purchas'd. I could wish
My birth were more obscure, my friends and kinsmen
Of lesser power, or that my provident father
Had been like to that riotous emperor
That chose his belly for his only heir;
For being of no family then, and poor,
My virtues, whereso'er I liv'd, should make
That kingdom my inheritance.

[GUIOMAR (*to Manuel*).   Strange self love!]

For if I studied the country's laws,
I should so easily sound all their depth,
And rise up such a wonder that the pleaders

That now are in most practice and esteem
Should starve for want of clients. If I travell'd
Like wise Ulysses, to see men and manners,
I would return in act more knowing than
Homer could fancy him. If a physician,
So oft I would restore death-wounded men
That where I liv'd Galen should not be nam'd,
And he that join'd again the scatter'd limbs
Of torn Hippolytus should be forgotten.
I could teach Ovid courtship, how to win
A Julia and enjoy her, though her dower
Were all the sun gives light to. And for arms,
Were the Persian host that drank up rivers added
To the Turk's present powers, I could direct,
Command and marshal them. **99**

GLOSSARY

pleaders advocates, barristers
Ulysses (Odysseus) the voyaging hero of Homer's *Odyssey*
fancy portray
Galen celebrated Greek physician
he that join'd again the . . . limbs of torn Hippolytus i.e. Asclepius, the
    Greek god of medicine, who restored Prince Hippolytus to life
    when he was torn apart by his horses after repulsing the amorous
    advances of his stepmother Phedra
Ovid Roman love-poet, whose 'Amores' were addressed to . . .
. . . *Julia* daughter of the Emperor Augustus, who banished Ovid from
    Rome.
the Persian host i.e. the vast army of Xerxes the Great in 480 BC

The Changeling
Thomas Middleton and William Rowley (1622)

WHO ☞ *De Flores, servant to Vermandero, the Governor of the Castle of Alicante, Spain. His name literally means 'de-flowerer'. 20s plus.*

WHERE ☞ *In the Castle of Alicante, Spain.*

TO WHOM ☞ *An aside to himself, though in the presence of Beatrice, as he is watching her.*

WHEN ☞ *Contemporary with authorship.*

WHAT HAS JUST HAPPENED ☞ *Beatrice is to marry Alonso but has fallen in love with the gentleman Alsemero. She needs help to remove Alonso from the picture – to have him murdered – and though she loathes the hideous De Flores, he is just the man for the job. But De Flores is infatuated by Beatrice to the point of stalking her. He is here watching her just before she asks for his help, which incidentally he agrees upon, on the condition that in payment he takes her virginity.*

WHAT HE WANTS/OBJECTIVES TO PLAY ☞

- *To let the audience know the extent of his masochistic obsession with her and the extent of her revulsion for him.*

- *To educate the audience – though he is a servant, he was born a gentleman.*

- *To communicate his confusion over why, though he is physically unattractive, there are others who look far worse and yet have some sort of love life.*

- *To assert his latent control, to let the audience know he is not the weak and powerless being he might seem – certainly that is how others perceive him in the play.*

NOTE ON THE TEXT ☞

[. . .] *indicates excluded dialogue between Beatrice and De Flores where Beatrice's contempt for him is reiterated.*

De Flores

" Yonder's she;
Whatever ails me, now o' late especially,
I can as well be hang'd as refrain seeing her;
Some twenty times a day, nay, not so little,
Do I force errands, frame ways and excuses,
To come into her sight; and I've small reason for't,
And less encouragement; for she baits me still
Every time worse than other, does profess herself
The cruellest enemy to my face in town,
At no hand can abide the sight of me,
As if danger or ill luck hung in my looks.
I must confess my face is bad enough,
But I know far worse has better fortune,
And not endur'd alone, but doted on;
And yet such pick-hair'd faces, chins like witches',
Here and there five hairs, whispering in a corner,
As if they grew in fear one of another,
Wrinkles like troughs, where swine-deformity swills
The tears of perjury that lie there like wash
Fallen from the slimy and dishonest eye –
Yet such a one plucks sweets without restraint,
And has the grace of beauty to his sweet.
Though my hard fate has thrust me out to servitude,
I tumbled into the world a gentleman.
She turns her blessèd eye upon me now,
And I'll endure all storms before I part with't. [. . .]

Why, am not I an ass, to devise ways
Thus to be rail'd at? I must see her still.
I shall have a mad qualm within this hour again,
I know't; and like a common Garden-bull,
I do but take breath to be lugg'd again.
What this may bode I know not; I'll despair the less,
Because there's daily precedents of bad faces
Belov'd beyond all reason; these foul chops
May come into favour one day, 'mongst his fellows;
Wrangling has prov'd the mistress of good pastime:

As children cry themselves asleep, I ha' seen
Women have chid themselves abed to men. **99**

force . . . frame contrive
baits torments
at no hand on no account
pick-hair'd sparsely bearded
wash tears, swill
has the grace of beauty to his sweet can boast a gracefully beautiful
    woman as his sweetheart
rail'd at verbally abused
mad qualm sharp pang (of lust)
Garden-bull i.e. a bull baited for entertainment in Southwark's Paris
    Garden
lugg'd pulled, tugged, baited
foul chops ugly features
have chid themselves abed to men have ended up in bed with the men
    they insult

The Roman Actor

Philip Massinger (1626)

WHO ☞ *Emperor Domitianus Caesar. 30's plus. A tyrannical and insanely jealous man.*

WHERE ☞ *In Caesar's palace, Rome, which under the rule of this emperor, has sunk to appalling depths. Citizens fear for their lives, with safety lying only in obeying the self-indulgent desires of the Emperor who considers himself a God.*

TO WHOM ☞ *The princesses – Julia (the Emperor's niece), Domitilla (his cousin) and Caenis (his deceased father's mistress); and Aretinus, a spy.*

WHEN ☞ AD *82.*

WHAT HAS JUST HAPPENED ☞ *In his arrogance, Caesar forced a divorce upon Domitia from her then husband in order that she become his Empress. He has since favoured her above the other princesses, which has caused them to hate her. But each of them also lives in fear of Domitian's cruelty, which is becoming more extreme. However, together with Aretinus, they have discovered evidence of Domitia's infidelity with the Roman actor of the title, Paris. They present Caesar with a signed testimony showing hard evidence of his wife's passion for the tragedian.*

WHAT HE WANTS/OBJECTIVES TO PLAY ☞

- *To let them know that he will not judge Domitia until he sees her and tests her himself, and that he prizes her honour above theirs collectively. He is humiliated by what he hears and has to respond from a position of defence.*

- *To build her up in their eyes, to encourage them to reappraise their findings if needs be.*

- *To warn them of the enormity of the accusation – their lives are at stake if they have got this wrong.*

- *To make them feel worthless and insignificant – and entirely dispensable.*

Domitianus Caesar

❝ I stand doubtful
And unresolv'd what to determine of you.
In this malicious violence you have offer'd
To the altar of her truth, and pureness to me,
You have but fruitlessly labour'd to sully
A white robe of perfection black-mouth'd envy
Could belch no spot on. But I will put off
The deity you labour to take from me,
And argue out of probabilities with you,
As if I were a man. Can I believe
That she that borrows all her light from me,
And knows to use it, would betray her darkness
To you that are her slaves, and therefore hate her,
Whose aids she might employ to make way for her?
Or Aretinus, whom long since she knew
To be the cabinet counsellor, nay, the key,
Of Caesar's secrets? Could her beauty raise her
To this unequall'd height, to make her fall
The more remarkable?
Or she leave our imperial bed to court
A public actor?

[ARETINUS.   Who dares contradict
These more than human reasons, that have power
To clothe base guilt in the most glorious shape
Of innocence?
DOMITILLA. Too well she knew the strength
And eloquence of her patron to defend her,
And thereupon presuming, fell securely,
Not fearing an accuser.]

                    I'll not hear
A syllable more that may invite a change
In my opinion of her. You have rais'd
A fiercer war within me by this fable
(Though with your lives you vow to make it history)
Than if, and at one instant, all my legions
Revolted from me, and came arm'd against me.

Here in this paper are the swords predestin'd
For my destruction; here the fatal stars
That threaten more than ruin; this the death's head
That does assure me, if she can prove false,
That I am mortal, which a sudden fever
Would prompt me to believe, and faintly yield to.
But now in my full confidence what she suffers,
In that, from any witness but myself,
I nourish a suspicion she's untrue,
My toughness returns to me. Lead on, monsters,
And by the forfeit of your lives confirm
She is all excellence, as you all baseness;
Or let mankind, for her fall, boldly swear
There are no chaste wives now, nor ever were. **99**

French and Spanish Golden Age

The golden era of Elizabethan and Jacobean drama was matched by a similarly rich Golden Age on the continent.

Spain was a country only recently defeated in war – and this had a notable effect on the writing of the time. It was nationalistic, principled and preoccupied with conduct, morality and integrity.

In Catholic France, actors were social outcasts, even denied a Christian burial. But its accomplishments between 1630 and 1680 lifted French theatre to an unrivalled pre-eminence in Europe, and kept it there throughout the eighteenth century. The comedies deal broadly with urban hypocrisy and small-time domestic villainy, drawing from the physical comedy and stereotypes of the *Commedia dell'Arte*. Rather than provoking belly laughs, these comedies, especially Molière's, are described by one contemporary critic as *'rire dans l'âme'* – or laughter in the soul.

The tragedies also deal with archetypes but on a grander scale, with the epic and timeless issues that underpin the very lives and aspirations of the pre-Republic French: honour, truth and faithfulness to the ruler. Many of the plots go back to Greek drama for inspiration, and the genre is truly neo-classical in its aspiration. Unlike Molière's verse, Racine's is lofty, grand and morally elevating, in both tone and form.

Like much of the English work, this period of European writing was characterised by a particularly vivid – almost physical – lyricism, a poetic language. Much of the verse was written in rhyming couplets. Today, this form carries little weight in the theatre and is best encountered in pantomimes or Gilbert and Sullivan operettas. In Golden Age France and Spain, the couplet carried the linguistic and emotional weight of the iambic pentameter, and shouldn't be ignored.

Peribanez

Lope de Vega (c. 1605-12), *adapt. Tanya Ronder*

WHO ☞ *Peribanez, a farmer. Casilda's husband. Late 20s plus.*

WHERE ☞ *A painter's house in the province of Toledo, Spain.*

TO WHOM ☞ *The audience.*

WHEN ☞ *Contemporary with authorship.*

WHAT HAS JUST HAPPENED ☞ *Peribanez is married to Casilda, who has attracted the attention of the local military commander, Don Fadrique; Don Fadrique's increasingly desperate attempts to win her finally lead him to make Peribanez a gentleman and army captain, in order to send him to war and away from Casilda and his home in Ocana. Whilst away Peribanez realises he has been coerced into the situation – he is staying at a painter's house, the very same painter who is working on Casilda's portrait for the Don. Having worked things out he decides to return home immediately.*

WHAT HE WANTS/OBJECTIVES TO PLAY ☞

- *To go back in time with the new-found knowledge that he has been duped by his own commander.*

- *To summon the courage to confront what he fears may be the reality of the situation back home.*

- *To torment himself with the possible repercussions of the situation.*

- *To doubt his worthiness of Casilda.*

- *To let himself off the hook at times – she is so beautiful this was bound to happen sooner or later.*

Peribanez

66 Backwards, go backwards, time unravel. Please not my mind, oh God. Don Fadrique has a painting of my wife. Just that leaves me sliced open to the vultures. But if she didn't know – does she not know? – maybe nobody knows. Maybe nobody knows. This is the cost of her beauty. Is the price of peace to marry a wife you don't love? He's robbed me of my peace, dear God. Casilda, my Queen. This is so ugly, this jealousy. I don't want it to be seen, I don't want anyone to know what he wants, what he wants to do with her. It's like he's had her already. Chewed her up and spat her out. I have to stop. He should protect me – he's my Lord. I serve him – he offers me honour and I serve him – not splay me open this way, hounded out of my home by laughter and contempt. If I leave Ocana, start a new life far from this nightmare, how will I live without my farm? Can I start again with nothing? I can't creep quietly back to my farm and home amongst whispers and gossip – everything I loved becomes my enemy. I need to talk to Casilda. Is she more than I deserve? What a stupid man I am. How could I think she could have been mine? That she was mine? How stupid to think that powerful wealth wouldn't want her too. Flick his envious eyes over her sweet face. Where would he flick his tongue? This will kill me. If this is what paint does, the real thing will send me to Hell. Christ! Help me, Saint Roque. I can't live with this. God protect me I'll kill him. Stupid, stupid, why was I so stupid? **99**

GLOSSARY

Saint Roque the patron saint against plague and disease

The Dog in the Manger

Lope De Vega (c. 1613), *trans. Jill Booty*

WHO ☞   *Tristán, servant to Teodoro, any age.*

WHERE ☞   *A room in the Countess's palace, Naples.*

TO WHOM ☞   *Teodoro, the Countess's secretary.*

WHEN ☞   *Contemporary with authorship.*

WHAT HAS JUST HAPPENED ☞ *Teodoro is having a secret relationship with Marcela, lady-in-waiting to Diana, the Countess of Balfour. Though she has suitors of her own, Diana has become obsessively jealous. Teodoro's servant, Tristán, is aware they are both in a dangerous and precarious position. In this speech, they have both narrowly escaped being discovered by Diana, whilst fleeing her apartments after a liaison with Marcela; Tristán tries to make Teodoro see sense and to stop seeing Marcela, for both their safety's and livelihoods' sakes.*

WHAT HE WANTS/OBJECTIVES TO PLAY ☞

- *To persuade him to fall out of love with Marcela.*
- *To offer a lesson in the passing of love.*
- *To disillusion him, albeit in a charm offensive.*
- *To diffuse the situation through laughter, after what has been a really close shave.*

Tristán

❝ A philosopher once said that the best part of beauty is a good tailor. So, do not imagine her leaning over her balcony looking so slim and elegant in all her finery, with a golden girdle about her waist, and high heeled shoes. All that is nothing but so much architecture. No. When you think of her, imagine her as a sinner in a penitent's robe. She will not look so enticing without her embroidered skirts and trimmings. In short, remember all her faults and you will soon find there is no better cure for love. Just think how, if you witness a repulsive and nauseating spectacle, it may put you off your food for a month. So, every time you think of her, think of something repellent about her, and that is your cure.

[TEODORO. What a vulgar, rustic remedy, and a crude surgeon! Your panaceas are such as I should have expected from your rough hand. You are a quack, Tristán, you know nothing of the art. I could never imagine a woman that way. I can only see them all as pure, beautiful, and clear as crystal.]

All their promises are as easily broken, that is the only likeness I can see. But it is quite clear, sir, that you are determined not to use my remedy and not to forget her. I was in love once myself, I swear it, an old bag of lies she was too, and fifty if she was a day. Now among some two thousand or so defects she had, the most apparent was the size of her belly. It could have held all the heaps of paper and rubbish piled upon any five hundred desks in the country, and still leave room for a few small architectural constructions here and there – bridges, parapets, palisades, and that sort of thing. Or if you prefer a classical turn of phrase, it could have held as many Greeks as the Trojan horse. Did you never hear of that famous walnut tree, in some village or other, which was so big that a poor clerk and his wife and family lived comfortably in its hollow trunk without being squeezed? Well, a weaver and his wife and family and loom could have lived in comfort inside that stomach of hers. Now, it so happened that I wanted to forget her – you can well understand that I might – so, instead of letting my imagination run away with me, and thinking of her in terms of lilies, jasmine, and orange blossom, of ivory, silver and snow all veiled by that fair curtain – her skirt – I kept a short rein on myself and thought of her in more suitable terms. I envisaged baskets full of mouldy pumpkins, old battered hampers, dirty linen chests, postmen's pouches loaded with letters, sacks full of old mattresses, bedding and bundles of old rags. Well, after a few such exercises of the imagination, all my love and hope turned to hatred and disdain. I forgot her, belly and all, for ever and ever, amen. And that was no small task, I assure you, for you could have packed four pestles into the folds of her flesh. But enough. I have made my point. **99**

GLOSSARY

parapets, palisades battlements, defensive fortifications
as many Greeks as the Trojan horse i.e. the wooden horse, packed with
    armed soldiers, by which the besieging Greek army gained entrance
    to the city of Troy

Life is a Dream

Pedro Calderón de la Barca (c. 1630), *trans. John Clifford*

WHO ☞ *Basilio, a King – described as 'an old man' by the author, but he could feasibly be in his 40s.*

WHERE ☞ *In the court.*

TO WHOM ☞ *Basilio is here addressing his nephew and niece, Astolfo and Estrella, and the court as he lays out his grand plan.*

WHEN ☞ *In a non-specific and mystical time, with medieval resonance.*

WHAT HAS JUST HAPPENED ☞ *The horoscope of the child prince Segismundo convinced his father, the Polish King and astrologer Basilio, that his son was destined to bring dishonour and downfall to Poland. He announced that Segismundo had died with his mother in birth and confined him in a tower, deep in the mountains, chaining him to a ring in the floor. Here, Basilio convenes an emergency session to explain to the court the history of his lost son, the reason why he has now brought him back to court and his plan for the future. This speech sets his plan up.*

WHAT HE WANTS/OBJECTIVES TO PLAY ☞

- *To rouse their pity for his predicament.*

- *To enthuse them with this plan.*

- *To get them to trust him implicitly – what he is revealing is of enormous importance, and he has lied to the court already in saying his son was dead. He needs to win their trust back.*

- *To remind them of his impressive credentials as an astronomer, let alone as a King.*

Basilio

66 The sciences I love the most
And engage in with a subtle and discerning mind
Are those which foretell the future,
Which steal the function of passing time
To tell us what happens with each day that comes.
For I can look at astrological tables
And I can foresee the future in the present.
The planets revolve in circles of snow,
The stars spread out a canopy of diamonds:
These are the subjects of my studies,
The sky is like a book to me, a book
Of diamond paper, with sapphire binding,
Written in letters of gold hieroglyphics
I can read and easily decipher. And so I know
What the future holds for each of us, for good or bad.
But I wish to God that my own life
Had been the first target of heaven's anger,
Long before I learnt to interpret its messages
And learnt to understand its signs.
For when a man is unfortunate
Even his gifts stab him in the back
And a man whose knowledge harms him
Murders his own self! This I can tell you,
Though in the events of my sad life
It is still better told.
So once again
It is for silence that I ask you.
Clorilene my wife gave birth to a son.
The omens of his birth were so many, and so dreadful
They exhausted the skies. While the baby still lay
In the womb's living grave, far from the beautiful light
Of day, she dreamt again and again of her belly torn open
By a monster in the shape of a man.
And on the day that he was born, the sun itself
Engaged in blood-soaked battle with the moon
With the earth as the battlefield. This was the worst eclipse

The world has suffered since weeping for the death of Christ.
The sun was smothered in living fire,
The heavens darkened, palaces trembled,
The clouds rained stones and the rivers ran with torrents
    of blood.
And it was under this sign
My son Segismundo was born.
He foretold his future in the manner of his birth,
For in being born he killed his mother
And so boasted with male ferocity:
'Look: I am human and this is how
We humans repay those who do us good.'
I ran to my books, and in them I read
Segismundo would be the most brutal man,
The cruellest prince, the most vicious monarch;
That under him his kingdom would become
Divided, split, torn by civil wars:
I saw him inspired by fury.
I saw him driven on by rage.
I saw him defeat and overcome me.
I saw me lying vanquished at his feet.
I saw me humiliated, helpless,
And forced to be his wretched slave. [. . .]

I had to believe such frightening predictions
I had to try to avert the evil that seemed sure to come.
I had to see if wisdom can help a human overcome the stars.
So I prepared a tower, hidden in the mountains,
Where the daylight scarcely dares enter.
I passed strict laws and edicts,
I forbade anyone to enter
And I had it announced that the prince was born dead.
There Segismundo lives, chained like a beast,
Imprisoned in poverty and misery. [. . .]

Three things must be considered here. The first
That I love my country, and I must do all I can
To rescue it from the prospect of a cruel vindictive king.
The second is that we are talking of my son.
He has the right to freedom, he has the right to rule.

To deprive him of these rights would be a crime,
A crime I cannot justify,
Even if what I intend is the good of all.
The third is that we know we should not too easily believe
That what is predicted will unavoidably occur.
Even the most evil omen, even the worst horoscope
Can only incline the will. It cannot force it.
And so my friends you must imagine me
Struggling for many months with these dilemmas
Until today, when I have finally found
A solution that will utterly amaze you. **99**

Don Juan

Molière (1665), trans. Kenneth McLeish

WHO ☞ *Don Juan. He is history's greatest cad and man about town, his name synonymous with seduction and sensuality. 20s plus.*

WHERE ☞ *In a town square, or any other public place.*

TO WHOM ☞ *Sganarelle, his servant.*

WHEN ☞ *Contemporary with authorship.*

WHAT HAS JUST HAPPENED ☞ *Don Juan has recently abducted Dona Elvira from a convent, and married her, so he could have his way with her. Growing tired of her charms, he is about to abandon her to attempt to seduce the fiancée of a friend. Sganarelle, his trusted and eminently more sensible servant, disapproves of his treatment of his 'wife'. This is Don Juan's response.*

WHAT HE WANTS/OBJECTIVES TO PLAY ☞

- *To set out his philosophy, namely, that he is a connoisseur not just of single beauty but also of all beauty. That his pleasure is in the chase, in the seduction, and that a permanent relationship would crush him.*

- *To seduce Sganarelle into this way of thinking in order to get him on side.*

- *To reduce the accepted 'honourable' way of behaviour to mere formality.*

- *To aggrandise himself by portraying his life in military terms, in order to emphasise the technical skill involved in his conquests and align himself with the heroes of the time.*

Don Juan

" So what *ought* people to do? Shackle themselves to the first one who catches their eye? Give up the whole world for her, never look at another living soul? What is that, some kind of chivalry? Wear the same suit of clothes from adolescence onwards; cut yourself off from all other changes and fashions in tailoring? Only fools are faithful. The Earth is full of pretty women, and just because one of them happens to be first, that's no reason to ignore the others. It's wrong to have favourites. Beauty snares me, wherever I find it, chains of roses, and I submit, I let it happen. I devote myself to them, one at a time, exclusively – but that doesn't stop me looking at what else is on offer. What are eyes for? I see their good points, the gifts Nature's given them – and pay them the compliment of appreciating them. My heart was made to love everything that's lovable – and when a pretty face demands that heart, I give it gladly. If I'd ten thousand hearts, I'd give them all. No pleasure on Earth can equal the first stirrings of passion, every single time, and the best thing about an affair is that it doesn't last. It's a siege, a military campaign, and that's the fun of it. You see a pretty girl, you start your manoeuvres . . . Every day a small advance . . . She's shy, she's inexperienced, she offers you such pretty resistance, such sweet little ploys, defences, and you find a thousand ways – tears, declarations, sighs – to make her learn to trust you. Gradually, gently, you make her forget the lessons she learned at her mother's knee . . . Slowly, patiently, you lead her just where you want her. But after that, what's left? What have you to say to her, or she to you? The battle's won. 'True and lasting love' is a quicksand, and if we fall into it, we die. Instead, some other sweet little creature happens along and the whole thing starts again. Conquering beauty is like conquering anything else – and what general was ever satisfied with a single triumph? I'm like Alexander the Great: I love the whole world. I want it, and when I've won it, I'll fall on my knees and beg new worlds to conquer. **"**

Phedra

Jean Racine (1677), trans. Julie Rose

WHO ☞ *Theseus, son of Aegeus and King of Athens, a renowned warrior and husband to Phedra. 40s.*

WHERE ☞ *A room in the royal palace, Athens.*

TO WHOM ☞ *His son, Hippolytus.*

WHEN ☞ *Racine took this Greek myth, and adapted it for his own time, though the setting is still very much the Athens of 7th century* BC.

WHAT HAS JUST HAPPENED ☞ *Phedra has fallen madly in love with her step-son, Hippolytus. Believing her husband to have been slain when warring away from home, she propositioned him. He rejected her, in no uncertain terms. In the meantime her husband Theseus has returned alive and well, and fearing Hippolytus would tell what she had done, she falsely accuses him of trying to assault her. Theseus is incandescent with rage, and is heartbroken that his son should have done this. It does not occur to him to doubt his wife's story of an attempted rape. His son has just arrived to welcome him back.*

WHAT HE WANTS/OBJECTIVES TO PLAY ☞

- *To annihilate him.*

- *To disown him, with scorn, revulsion and loathing.*

- *To find the generosity to give him some chance of life by allowing him to escape.*

- *To condemn him, adding the gods' damnation to his own.*

Theseus

❝ Traitor! You dare show yourself to me?
Monster! You should have been struck by lightning long ago!
I must have missed you when I purged the earth

Of the last of its vile scum!
You dare show your face to me
Here in this place you've polluted
With your ghastly love – this lust
That drove you as far as your own father's bed!
Go! Crawl under a rock! Hide
Somewhere far away
Where no-one's heard of Theseus
Or who he is, or what you are!
Don't brave my hate again,
Or tempt the fury I can barely contain.
Fathering a son like you
Has brought me shame enough
Without your death tarnishing my memory,
And dinting the glory of my noble deeds.
Get right away, unless you want to die
Like the other mongrel dogs I've happily dispatched.
Take care the sun that lights our days
Never catches you with your foot on this soil again.
Go, I say; go as fast as you can, and never turn back,
Purge my realm of your stinking presence.
And you, Neptune, if I have, in the past,
Cleared your coasts of infamous assassins,
Remember, to reward a successful campaign,
You promised to grant my one most fervent wish.
In all the long hard months in prison
I never once called on you.
I saved your mercy for more pressing needs.
I implore you now, Neptune. Revenge a wronged father.
This traitor I abandon to your unremitting rage.
Quench the obscene fires in his blood.
I'll recognise your power by the fury of your revenge.

[HIPPOLYTUS. Phedra accuses me of a criminal love!
Horror numbs my soul;
Unexpected blows rain down on me.
I can't breathe. My voice has dried up.]

Traitor, you thought she'd be scared into silence
And this would bury your shameless brutality!

Pity that in your flight you left behind, in her hands,
The sword that overwhelmingly condemns you!
You should have gone the whole way
And with one thrust silenced her and killed her. **99**

GLOSSARY

Neptune the god of the sea

Restoration and Eighteenth Century

The Restoration refers to the 'restoration' of the monarchy,
the return of Charles II from exile in France, and the end of
the Puritan stranglehold on the arts. Theatres that had been
closed were reopened, while new ones were built. Indoor
theatres grew in popularity, which changed the whole ambience
and atmosphere of playgoing, with candlelit evening
performances becoming the norm.

The acting became more playful than before, less declamatory,
less epic, and gave birth to the domestic 'comedy of
manners', investigating, commenting on and criticising
a new, licentious world. Wit and wordplay were the most
obvious characteristics of the new theatrical language.
Themes included the rural idyll of the country against the
cynical and superficial town, the corruption of innocence,
the social necessity of marrying for property rather than
love, and the consequent eruption of adultery.

The Restoration was about sex, and the playing of its
delicious language is like sport – a blood sport! Treat the text
like a musical score: play it exactly as it is written in terms
of its sentence structure, and don't under- or overplay the
running motifs or cunning *double entendres*.

Body language was just as important as anything spoken, and
a complex system of pointers and signs was established. The
lady's fan was not so much a tool for cooling herself as a
highly sophisticated communication device. By fanning
herself slowly a woman meant 'I am married'; fanning
quickly and she was engaged; and twirling the fan in the
right hand meant 'I love another'.

Eighteenth-century writing replaced the Restoration's bawdy
overtones with a much more genteel sensibility, but the
comedy of manners reached another highpoint in Sheridan,
from whom there is a direct line through to the comedies of
Oscar Wilde and Noël Coward. The language is decidedly

more accessible than the Restoration. It almost feels modern, though it still has that period colour, verve and sharpness of wit.

The eighteenth century was a romantic, morally reformative era of society and creativity, bridging the gap between the Restoration and the highground of Victorian manners. Within the drama of this period there was a sneaking sense of the censorious melodrama to come, the beginnings of a complete reversal of Restoration values – or lack of them.

The Man of Mode

George Etherege (1676)

WHO ☞ *An actor, out of character, any age.*

WHERE ☞ *On stage, after the curtain call.*

TO WHOM ☞ *The audience.*

WHEN ☞ *Contemporary with authorship.*

WHAT HAS JUST HAPPENED ☞ *This is the epilogue of the play, spoken by an actor of the company, out of character. The epilogue serves as a cautionary rounding off to the story, a full stop to the events. He is talking to the audience about the convention of the Restoration fop – a man given over to the finer things in life, an aesthete, devoted to the materialistic exquisite and to women. He uses Sir Fopling Flutter, the dandy of this play, to illustrate.*

WHAT HE WANTS/OBJECTIVES TO PLAY ☞

- *To entertain and enlighten the audience and to flatter their intellect and their sensibilities.*
- *To differentiate between the true fop and the one that is predatory: he who takes something that he likes from every man, and adopts it as his own.*
- *To warn that the latter type of fop ultimately comes to represent all the men in the shire, as he is made up of the parts of them – so beware!*

Dryden

“ Most modern wits such monstrous fools have shown,
They seem'd not of heaven's making but their own.
Those nauseous harlequins in farce may pass,
But there goes more to a substantial ass.
Something of man must be expos'd to view,
That, gallants, they may more resemble you.

Sir Fopling is a fool so nicely writ,
The ladies would mistake him for a wit.
And when he sings, talks loud, and cocks, would cry,
'I vow methinks he's pretty company!'
So brisk, so gay, so travell'd, so refin'd,
As he took pains to graft upon his kind.
True fops help nature's work, and go to school,
To file and finish God Almighty's fool.
Yet none Sir Fopling him, or him can call;
He's knight o'th' shire, and represents ye all.
From each he meets he culls whate'er he can,
Legion's his name, a people in a man.
His bulky folly gathers as it goes,
And, rolling o'er you, like a snowball grows.
His various modes from various fathers follow,
One taught the toss, and one the new French wallow.
His sword-knot this, his cravat this design'd,
And this the yard-long snake he twirls behind.
From one the sacred periwig he gain'd,
Which wind ne'er blew, nor touch of hat profan'd.
Another's diving bow he did adore,
Which with a shog casts all the hair before:
Till he with full decorum brings it back
And rises with a water-spaniel shake.
As for his songs (the ladies' dear delight)
Those, sure, he took from most of you who write.
Yet every man is safe from what he fear'd,
For no one fool is hunted from the herd. **99**

GLOSSARY

harlequins painted clowns
cocks struts
graft upon his kind inspire emulation in his fellows
file refine
knight o'th' shire representative in Parliament
sword-knot elaborate ribbon tied to a gentleman's scabberd
toss . . . wallow swagger of the head . . . rolling gait
snake the voluminous tail of a full-bottom wig
diving bow ostentatious act of obeisance
shog shake

The Rover

Aphra Behn (1677)

WHO ☞   *Blunt, a young country gentleman, described in the play as a wealthy 'Essex calf', 20s.*

WHERE ☞   *In a street in Naples during carnival.*

TO WHOM ☞   *The audience.*

WHEN ☞   *1650s.*

WHAT HAS JUST HAPPENED ☞   *Captain Willmore (the 'rover' of the title) has stepped ashore in search of 'love and mirth' and is met by his friends from England, one of whom is Blunt. During the carnival jollity he has been seduced by a wench, Lucetta, and lured to her home for recreation. However, as soon as he was undressed she set off a trap, dropping him into a sewer, so she could steal his belongings. Blunt reappears from the sewer in this soliloquy, in his underwear and besmirched with filth. He is furious.*

WHAT HE WANTS/OBJECTIVES TO PLAY ☞

- *To rage against all women!*

- *To take pity on himself for being so gullible and so stupid – he wasn't even drunk.*

- *To get back to his lodgings with as much dignity as he can muster in his current state.*

Blunt

❝ Oh Lord, I am got out at last, and, which is a miracle, without a clue. And now to damning and cursing! But if that would ease me, where shall I begin? With my fortune, myself, or the quean that cozened me? What a dog was I to believe in woman! Oh, coxcomb! Ignorant conceited coxcomb! To fancy she could be enamoured with my person! At first sight enamoured! Oh, I'm a cursed puppy! 'Tis plain, 'fool' was writ upon my forehead! She perceived it; saw the Essex calf there. For what allurements could there be in this countenance, which I can endure because I'm acquainted with it. Oh dull, silly dog, to be thus soothed into a cozening! Had I been drunk, I might fondly have credited the young quean; but as I was in my right wits to be thus cheated, confirms it I am a dull, believing, English country fop. But my comrades! Death and the devil, there's the worst of all! Then a ballad will be sung tomorrow on the Prado, to a lousy tune of the Enchanted Squire and the Annihilated Damsel. But Fred – that rogue – and the Colonel will abuse me beyond all Christian patience. Had she left me my clothes, I have a bill of exchange at home would have saved my credit. But now all hope is taken from me. Well, I'll home, if I can find the way, with this consolation: that I am not the first kind, believing coxcomb; but there are, gallants, many such good natures amongst ye.

And though you've better arts to hide your follies, 'Adsheartlikins, y'are all as arrant cullies. **99**

GLOSSARY

quean hussy
cozened deceived
coxcomb fool
Essex calf country dolt
allurements temptations
on the Prado i.e. in the public square
bill of exchange receipt
'Adsheartikins God's little heart!
arrant notoriously without moderation
cullies dupes, gulls

The Relapse

John Vanbrugh (1696)

WHO ☞ *Loveless, a reformed libertine and gentleman.*

WHERE ☞ *In a London garden.*

TO WHOM ☞ *The audience.*

WHEN ☞ *Contemporary with authorship.*

WHAT HAS JUST HAPPENED ☞ *Loveless has been living in the country with his wife Amanda. Despite making a great show of being deeply in love with his wife, on the couple's return to London, Loveless returns to his former ways, pursuing the beautiful young widow, Berinthia, Amanda's cousin. In this soliloquy he muses on the nature of his relationship with each woman. With his sophisticated and witty style, Loveless is representative of the world of the play – one without principles and where outrageous behaviour is tolerated as long as it is conducted by the wealthy. The actor can particularly enjoy the transition from verse to prose as Loveless's instincts take hold and he proves himself morally redundant.*

WHAT HE WANTS/OBJECTIVES TO PLAY ☞

- *To offload the responsibility of his urges by putting the blame onto Fate.*

- *To shake himself out of what he is feeling by reminding himself of what he is beholden to his wife for – his salvation.*

- *To convince himself that what he feels for his wife is very different from what he feels for her cousin. They are different sorts of love.*

- *To get to the core of what this new attraction is about – he does not understand it.*

Loveless

❝ Sure, Fate has yet some business to be done,
Before Amanda's heart and mine must rest;
Else, why amongst those legions of her sex,
Which throng the world,
Should she pick out for her companion
The only one on earth
Whom nature has endow'd for her undoing?
Undoing, was't I said – who shall undo her?
Is not her empire fix'd? am I not hers?
Did she not rescue me, a grovelling slave,
When chain'd and bound by that black tyrant vice,
I labour'd in his vilest drudgery?
Did she not ransom me, and set me free?
Nay, more: when by my follies sunk
To a poor, tatter'd, despicable beggar,
Did she not lift me up to envied fortune?
Give me herself, and all that she possessed,
Without a thought of more return,
Than what a poor repenting heart might make her?
Han't she done this? And if she has,
Am I not strongly bound to love her for it?
To love her! – Why, do I not love her then?
By Earth and Heaven I do!
Nay, I have demonstration that I do:
For I would sacrifice my life to serve her.
Yet hold – if laying down my life
By demonstration of my love,
What is't I feel in favour of Berinthia?

For should she be in danger, methinks, I could incline to risk
it for her service too; and yet I do not love her. How then
subsists my proof? – Oh, I have found it out! What I would
do for one, is demonstration of my love; and if I'd do as
much for t'other, it there is demonstration of my friendship.
Ay, it must be so. I find I'm very much her friend. – Yet, let
me ask myself one puzzling question more. Whence springs
this mighty friendship all at once? For our acquaintance is of

later date. Now friendship's said to be a plant of tedious growth; its root composed of tender fibres, nice in their taste, cautious in spreading, checked with the last corruption in the soil; long ere it take, and longer still ere it appear to do so: whilst mine is in a moment shot so high, and fixed so fast, it seems beyond the power of storms to shake it. I doubt it thrives too fast. 99

GLOSSARY

nice delicate
ere before
doubt fear

The Beaux Stratagem

George Farquhar (1707)

WHO ☞   *Aimwell, a young impoverished gentleman,*
20s plus.

WHERE ☞   *A room in a country inn.*

TO WHOM ☞   *Archer, his friend.*

WHEN ☞   *Contemporary with authorship.*

WHAT HAS JUST HAPPENED ☞   *Aimwell and Archer are a
pair of poor but presentable London gentlemen who arrive at an
English country inn plotting to regain their fortunes. In
Aimwell's case, as is the law as younger son, he has been denied
his share in the family fortune. He plans to assume his older
brother's identity and so improve his chances of marrying a
wealthy woman. His friend Archer has agreed to act as
Aimwell's servant with the promise that he will receive half of
what Aimwell receives. Aimwell has set his sights on Dorinda, the
daughter of a wealthy local widow. They are fired up and about
to make their entrance at the local church. Here Aimwell
explains his strategy of seduction: deception.*

WHAT HE WANTS/OBJECTIVES TO PLAY ☞

- *To inspire his friend with a story of how it generally passes in
  such instances.*

- *To indulge and enjoy his belief that he really is terribly clever
  and cunning; believing he is a man 'in the know'; revelling in
  his sense of superiority to both Archer and the people he is yet
  to meet.*

- *To laugh with Archer at how simple and corruptible these
  country folk are.*

Aimwell

66 The appearance of a stranger in a country church draws as many gazers as a blazing star. No sooner he comes into the cathedral but a train of whispers runs buzzing round the congregation in a moment. 'Who is he? Whence comes he? Do you know him?' Then I, sir, tips me the Verger with half a crown; he pockets the simony, and inducts me into the best pew in the church; I pull out my snuffbox, turn myself round, bow to the Bishop – or the Dean, if he be the commanding officer – single out a beauty, rivet both my eyes to hers, set my nose a-bleeding by the strength of imagination, and show the whole church my concern, by endeavouring to hide it; after the sermon the whole town gives me to her for a lover, and by persuading the lady that I am a-dying for her, the tables are turned, and she in good earnest falls in love with me. 99

GLOSSARY

simony ecclesiastical bribe

The Tragedy of Jane Shore

Nicholas Rowe (1714)

WHO ☞   *Bellmour, friend to Jane Shore. 30s plus.*

WHERE ☞   *The street.*

TO WHOM ☞   *Dumont, Jane's ex-husband.*

WHEN ☞   *1480s.*

WHAT HAS JUST HAPPENED ☞   *It is a politically dangerous time. Edward IV has died, leaving his young son Edward, to take the throne. However, the Duke of Gloucester (the future Richard III) plans to take the throne. His only obstacle is Lord Hastings, former chamberlain to Edward IV. Gloucester needs evidence of Hastings's rivalry to 'remove' him from the scene, and it comes in an anonymous betrayal by Alicia, Hastings's lover and Jane's friend. Alicia mistakenly believes the two of them to have rekindled their previous relationship. She also implicates Jane as the power behind Hastings. Gloucester demands that Hastings is executed; Jane's punishment is to be turned on to the streets as a beggar. Jane has gone from famously honourable lady in mourning for her King and her love, to vagrant, in one fell swoop. And all unjustified. At this point Bellmour, Jane's friend, describes the pitiful sight of her wandering the streets.*

WHAT HE WANTS/OBJECTIVES TO PLAY ☞

- *To give Dumont all the information he needs before meeting up with his ex-wife.*

- *To arouse pity in Dumont.*

- *To make himself feel better – it is cathartic for Bellmour: painting this elaborate and painfully exquisite picture, and speaking it out loud, helps him better cope with the injustice of it all.*

Bellmour
❝   I met her as returning
In solemn penance from the public cross:
Before her certain rascal officers,

Slaves in authority, the knaves of justice,
Proclaimed the tyrant Gloucester's cruel orders.
On either side her march'd an ill-look'd priest,
Who with severe, with horrid haggard eyes,
Did ever and anon by turns upbraid her,
And thunder in her trembling ear damnation.
Around her, numberless the rabble flow'd,
Shrouding each other, crowding for a view,
Gaping and gazing, taunting and reviling;
Some pitying, but those, alas! How few!
The most, such iron hearts we are, and such
The base barbarity of human kind,
With insolence and lewd reproach pursued her,
Hooting and railing, and with villainous hands
Gathering the filth from out the common ways,
To hurl upon her head.

[SHORE.   Inhuman dogs!
How did she bear it?
BELMOUR   With the gentlest patience.]

Submissive, sad, and lowly was her look;
A burning taper in her hand she bore,
And on her shoulders carelessly confus'd
With loose neglect her lovely tresses hung;
Upon her cheek a faintish flush was spread;
Feeble she seemed, and sorely smit with pain,
While barefoot as she trod the flinty pavement,
Her footsteps all along were mark'd with blood.
Yet silent still she pass'd and unrepining;
Her streaming eyes bent ever on the earth,
Except when in some bitter pang of sorrow,
To Heaven she seemed in fervent zeal to raise,
And beg that mercy man denied her here. **99**

GLOSSARY

the public cross the market square
rascal officers dissolute constables
ill-look'd scowling
common ways gutters
tresses locks of hair
unrepining uncomplaining

The Provok'd Husband

John Vanbrugh and Colley Cibber (1728)

WHO ☞   *Lord Townley, late 20s plus.*

WHERE ☞   *In his apartment in London.*

TO WHOM ☞   *The audience.*

WHEN ☞   *Contemporary with authorship.*

WHAT HAS JUST HAPPENED ☞ *This is the opening speech of the play, and all that you need to know in terms of his marriage to this rather 'modern' woman is in the text.*

WHAT HE WANTS/OBJECTIVES TO PLAY ☞

- *To win the sympathy and compassion of the audience.*
- *To draw the courage from the listener to change the status quo.*
- *To condemn these modern women.*
- *To voice his indignation at the treatment he is receiving at the hands of his wife.*

Lord Townley

❝ Why did I marry? Was it not evident my plain, rational scheme of life was impracticable, with a woman of so different a way of thinking? Is there one article of it that she has not broke in upon? Yes, let me do her justice – her reputation; *that* I have no reason to believe is in question. But then, how long her profligate course of pleasures may make her able to keep it – is a shocking question! And her presumption while she keeps it – insupportable! For on the pride of that single virtue she seems to lay it down, as a fundamental point, that the free indulgence of every other vice this fertile town affords is the birthright prerogative of a woman of quality. Amazing, that a creature so warm in the pursuit of her pleasures should never cast one thought towards her happiness. Thus, while she admits no lover, she thinks it a greater merit still, in her chastity not to care for her husband; and while she herself is solacing in one continual round of cards and good company, he, poor wretch, is left at large to take care of his own contentment. 'Tis time, indeed, some care were taken, and speedily there shall be. Yet let me not be rash. Perhaps this disappointment of my heart may make me too impatient; and some tempers, when reproached, grow more untractable. – Here she comes. Let me be calm awhile. **99**

GLOSSARY

insupportable intolerable

The Rivals

Richard Brinsley Sheridan (1775)

WHO ☞ *Faulkland. A young gentleman, fiancé to Julia, 20s/early 30s.*

WHERE ☞ *In Julia's dressing room.*

TO WHOM ☞ *A monologue that changes focus: it is played to himself, to Julia, believing her still to be in earshot, and to the audience.*

WHEN ☞ *Contemporary with authorship.*

WHAT HAS JUST HAPPENED ☞ *Faulkland is engaged to Julia, whom he loves dearly. But he is a man so obsessively jealous that he feels he has to keep checking her devotion. So he relates invented tragic scenarios to observe her reaction; questions her every deed; finds the opportunity to argue the smallest point against her – he has been doing this for a year now, and it has certainly played a part in delaying their wedding day. This speech comes from two scenes. The first part is his response to her running distraught after a discussion in which he has accused her of enjoying herself far too much when she was in the country away from him. The second part comes after yet another invented tragic tale to test her love. On discovering this was another of his 'stories', she informs him he has gone too far and she leaves him, for good. Together the speeches can work as a whole if you play the emotional journey from a rather defensive persuasion for her to come back through to the realisation he has lost everything that means anything to him.*

WHAT HE WANTS/OBJECTIVES TO PLAY ☞

- *To persuade Julia back.*

- *To show the audience the wily ways and emotional tricks played by women.*

- *To make himself feel better about being so suspicious and at the same time to beat himself up for being so awful to her.*

- *To pull himself together, finally, to win back what he believes he has lost, the love of a good and a deserving woman.*

Faulkland

❝ In tears! Stay, Julia, stay but for a moment. – The door is fastened! – Julia! – my soul – but for one moment – I hear her sobbing! 'Sdeath! What a brute am I to use her thus! Yet stay – aye – she is coming now: how little resolution there is in woman! – how a few soft words can turn them! No, faith! – she is not coming either. Why, Julia – my love – say but that you forgive me – come but to tell me that – now, this is being too resentful: stay! she is coming too – I thought she would – no steadiness in anything! Her going away must have been a mere trick then – she shan't see that I was hurt by it. I'll affect indifference – (*Hums a tune; then listens.*) No – zounds! she's not coming! – nor don't intend it, I suppose. This is not steadiness, but obstinacy! Yet I deserve it. What, after so long an absence, to quarrel with her tenderness! – 'twas barbarous and unmanly! I should be ashamed to see her now. I'll wait till her just resentment is abated – and when I distress her so again, may I lose her for ever! and be linked instead to some antique virago, whose gnawing passions, and long-hoarded spleen, shall make me curse my folly half the day, and all the night! [. . .]

She's gone – for ever! – there was an awful resolution in her manner, that riveted me to my place. – O fool! – dolt! – barbarian! Cursed as I am, with more imperfections than my fellow wretches, kind Fortune sent a heaven-gifted cherub to my aid, and like a ruffian, I have driven her from my side! – I must now haste to my appointment. Well, my mind is tuned for such a scene. I shall wish only to become a principal in it, and reverse the tale my cursed folly put me upon forging here. – O Love! – tormentor! – fiend! – whose influence, like the moon's, acting on men of dull souls, makes idiots of them, but meeting subtler spirits, betrays their course, and urges sensibility to madness! **❞**

GLOSSARY

sdeath! . . . *zounds!* i.e. by God's death! . . . by God's wounds (mild
    expletives)
antique virago classic man-hater

A Trip to Scarborough

Richard Brinsley Sheridan (1777)

WHO ☞   *Lord Foppington, a London dandy.*

WHERE ☞   *In his friend Loveless's home in Scarborough.*

TO WHOM ☞   *He is addressing Amanda, the object of his desires, her husband, Loveless, and her cousin, the beautiful Berinthia – so a good audience for this showman.*

WHEN ☞   *Contemporary with authorship.*

WHAT HAS JUST HAPPENED ☞   *In this classic Restoration comedy of manners, Lord Foppington has come to the country, Scarborough, to marry an heiress, a marriage arranged for him by a matchmaker. The two have not yet even met. But the day before the wedding, Foppington has other things on his mind: the seduction of his friend Loveless's wife, the virtuous Amanda. She detests him and all he stands for, the superficiality and silliness of the London 'man of quality' or 'fop' – a man given to fripperies, fine dress and the cuckolding of so-called friends. Lord Foppington has just arrived at the Loveless household and, as a means of impressing and seducing Amanda, who has just told him that she loves the country and to read, regales her with his philosophy for fine living – describing what is a typical day for him; or so he says.*

WHAT HE WANTS/OBJECTIVES TO PLAY ☞

- *To impress the ladies, particularly Amanda.*
- *To educate these ladies from the country of what one should do in the 'tawn'.*
- *To dazzle them intellectually, not just with what he says but how he says it, with his rhetoric and his fashionable pronunciation.*

Lord Foppington

❝ I am so much of your ladyship's mind, Madam, that I have a private gallery in tawn, where I walk sometimes, which is furnished with nothing but books and looking-glasses. Madam, I have gilded them, and ranged them so prettily, before Gad, it is the most entertaining thing in the world, to walk and look at them. [. . .] I must confess, I am not altogether so fand of . . . the inside of the book . . . which is to entertain one's self with the forced product of another man's brain. Now I think a man of quality and breeding may be much more diverted with the natural sprauts of his own; but to say the truth, Madam, let a man love reading never so well, when once he comes to know the tawn, he finds so many better ways of passing away the four-and-twenty hours, that it were ten thousand pities he should consume his time in that. For example, Madam, now my life, my life, Madam, is a perpetual stream of pleasure, that glides through with such a variety of entertainments, I believe the wisest of our ancestors never had the least conception of any of 'em. I rise, Madam, when in tawn, about twelve o'clock. I don't rise sooner, because it is the worst thing in the world for the complexion; nat that I pretend to be a beau, but a man must endeavour to look decent, lest he makes so odious a figure in the side-bax, the ladies should be compelled to turn their eyes upon the play; so, at twelve o'clock I say I rise. Naw, if I find it a good day, I resolve to take the exercise of riding, so drink my chocolate, and draw on my boots by two. On my return, I dress, and after dinner, lounge, perhaps to the Opera [. . .] provided there is good company, and one is not expected to undergo the fatigue of listening [. . .] Why then, ladies, there only remains to add, that I generally conclude the evening at one or other of the clubs, nat that I ever play deep; indeed I have been for some time tied up from losing above five thousand pawnds at a sitting [. . .] as to weighty affairs, I leave them to weighty heads; I never intend mine shall be a burthen to my body. **99**

GLOSSARY
beau man-about-town
play deep take the game seriously

Nineteenth and Early Twentieth Centuries

Over the nineteenth and early twentieth centuries, theatre genres included spectacle and melodrama, politically conscious drama, acute social comedy and naturalism.

Melodrama is immediately identifiable as drama which deals primarily with morality. Characters are either good or bad, the issues either black or white; the stakes are always high; and musical accompaniment was the greatest character of all. Many films and much of television soap opera today abide by the principles of melodrama.

By contrast, in the works of Ibsen, Strindberg and Chekhov, nothing happens, seemingly – and yet everything happens. Their plays, written in the last quarter of the nineteenth century and the first years of the twentieth, are domestic in setting, but their themes are huge and primeval: love, loss, freedom (personal as well as national and civic), and death (of an era, or a place, as well as of a human being). The characters talk conversationally, apparently not saying much of significance, but everything is communicated between the words, in the pauses; the subtext is seething with often-unvoiced intentions.

There is an effusive, passionate and poetic element to this writing. The translations selected here reflect the everyday reality of the language, without losing the flavour and weight of the original. It is important not to listen to the latent poetic qualities, or be seduced by the lyricism. Play the text as accurately and in as truthful a way as possible. Stanislavski's system of acting was created to give actors a new way to approach precisely this sort of writing. In preparing these naturalistic speeches, attentive emotional investigation should help you excavate the rich subtext.

Oscar Wilde's work at the very end of the nineteenth century is different. His style developed the witticisms and verbal pyrotechnics of the eighteenth century – writing which looked underneath the polite veneer of society and revealed its shallowness. The sentences are long, the rhythms crucial, and to maximise the comic effect you should only take a breath on a full stop.

George Bernard Shaw takes a step further towards the politicisation of drama. Shaw was a socialist, a fantastically intellectual and liberal thinker, a modernist and a man preoccupied first and foremost with the hypocrisy of the contemporary world. His work heralded socially-conscious drama in Britain, and formed the perfect counterpoint to the trend of naturalism being pioneered in Russia and Scandinavia. His writing needs to be played as a musical score – if you change the punctuation, it will not be 'Shaw'.

Lorenzaccio

Alfred de Musset (1834), *trans. Donald Watson*

WHO ☞ *Lorenzo de Medici, cousin to the Duke of Florence. 20s plus.*

WHERE ☞ *A street in Florence.*

TO WHOM ☞ *To the audience.*

WHEN ☞ *1537.*

WHAT HAS JUST HAPPENED ☞ *Lorenzo of the Medici family has decided to murder his cousin and friend, the notorious Alexander de Medici, the Duke of Florence, in order to put a halt to his tyrannous rule. Calling himself a modern-day Brutus, he believes that only with this murder can Florence regain its freedom and dignity. However in order to win the Duke's trust, Lorenzo has had to pay a high price morally – living as equally promiscuously as the Duke himself. In this speech, he both laments the lecherous person he has had to become, and the rights and wrongs of the assassination about to take place.*

WHAT HE WANTS/OBJECTIVES TO PLAY ☞

- *To build his confidence for the task ahead of him.*

- *To question his own humanity – out loud – to relieve his sense of shame at his gradual degradation.*

- *To mourn the loss of his innocence.*

- *To voice his fear that though this is for the public good, there is no personal reason to take his life; that it is an unnatural act and will trigger unnatural consequences.*

Lorenzo

❝ When I was in my mother's womb, what tiger haunted her dreams? The spectre of myself when young, doting on flowers and fields and Petrarch's sonnets, rises before me,

shuddering in horror. Oh God! At the mere thought of
tonight, why does joy burn me like a red-hot brand, so I feel
it even in my bones? From what savage entrails am I sprung?
What monstrous coupling presided at my birth? What has he
done to me, this man? If, hand on heart, I'm honest with
myself – who can hear me say tomorrow 'I have killed him',
without asking why I did it? It's strange. Though he's done
wrong to others, at least after his fashion he has been good to
me. If I had quietly stayed in the deep solitude of
Cafaggiuolo, he would never have sought me out. Yet I came
to Florence in search of him. But why? Was it my father's
ghost urging me on, like Orestes, to track down a new
Aegisthus? What offence had he done me, then? It's strange,
yet for this, I gave up everything. The sole thought of this
murder has crumbled my whole life's dreams to dust. Once
this assassination stood like a sinister raven in my path,
luring me on, and as a man I was ruined. What can it all
mean? Just now, as I walked through the square, I heard two
men talking of a comet. What I feel here, beneath my ribs, is
this the beating of a human heart? Oh, why lately has this
question come to me so often? Am I the arm of God? Is
there some cloud of glory above my head? When I enter that
room about to draw my sword from its sheath, I fear it may
be the flaming sword of Archangel Michael and I turn to
ashes as I fall upon my prey. **99**

GLOSSARY

beau man-about-town

play deep take the game seriously *Petrarch's sonnets* i.e. the classic love
    poetry of the Italian Renaissance poet

Orestes . . . Aegisthus in Greek myth, Orestes revenged the murder of
    his father Agamemnon by his mother Clytemnestra and her lover
    Aegisthus.

talking of a comet discussing an astrological omen

the arm of God the instrument of God's vengeance

Archangel Michael the prince of the angels, personification of justice

The Government Inspector

Nikolai Gogol (1836), *trans. Stephen Mulrine*

WHO ☞ *Khlestakov, a young St Petersburg clerk, 20s.*

WHERE ☞ *A room in the Mayor's house, in a nameless, provincial town.*

TO WHOM ☞ *The Mayor, his wife and daughter and a host of local dignitaries.*

WHEN ☞ *Contemporary with authorship.*

WHAT HAS JUST HAPPENED ☞ *A young civil servant from Saint Petersburg, Khlestakov, is mistaken by the members of a small town for a high-ranking government inspector. The town's Mayor fears the consequences of a visit by a government inspector, should he observe the extent of their corruption. Khlestakov takes advantage of this mistake, boasting of his life as an important man. In this speech Khlestakov meets the Mayor's wife and daughter and his story becomes more elaborate to win over the daughter, whom he has taken a fancy to.*

WHAT HE WANTS/OBJECTIVES TO PLAY ☞

- *To impress them.*
- *To convince himself that this is all true, so to create it as he speaks it.*
- *To stay upright and cogent: he has been drinking heavily.*

Khlestakov

❝ And I know all the best-looking actresses. I write the odd vaudeville sketch you see, and I'm pretty well in with the literary types. Yes, Pushkin and I are like that. (*Crosses fingers.*) I often say to him: 'Well, Pushkin, old chap, how are things?' And he'll say: 'Oh, so–so, old boy, can't complain . . .' Yes, he's a real character. [. . .]

Yes, I must admit I simply live for literature. I have the very first house in St Petersburg, everybody knows it: Khlestakov's house. (*Turns to address them all.*) Gentlemen, if you're ever in St Petersburg, please, please, do me the kindness of calling on me. I give balls too, you know.

[ANNA. Oh, I can just imagine those balls, they must be magnificent, and so tasteful!]

They're beyond words, ma'am. Melons on the table, for instance – seven hundred roubles apiece. Soup shipped in direct from Paris, still in the pot – you lift the lid, and the aroma, well, it's just out of this world! And I'm out at a ball every evening. We get up our own little whist party: the Foreign Minister, the French Ambassador, the English and German Ambassadors, and myself. You can practically kill yourself playing cards, you wouldn't believe it. I mean, you run up the stairs to the fourth floor, and you can just about manage to say to the cook: 'Here, Mavra, old girl, take my coat . . . ' What am I talking about? I've forgotten I live on the first floor! My staircase alone must be worth, oh . . . And you should see my waiting-room, even before I'm up, it's a sight to behold – counts and princes, all buzzing around, bumping into each other, like a swarm of bees, that's all you hear – buzz–buzz–buzz . . . Now and again the Minister himself . . . I even get parcels addressed to 'Your Excellency'. I was in charge of the department once too – an odd business, the Director went off somewhere, Lord knows where, and of course, there was a lot of talk about who should take over. Generals and everything volunteered for the job, but when it came to the bit, well, they just weren't up to it. It's not as easy as it looks, by God, it's not! Anyway, there was nothing else for it, they could see that, they had to send for me. So next minute the streets were full of messengers, running all over the place – thirty-five thousand messengers, would you believe! 'What's the problem?' I ask. 'Ivan Aleksandrovich, please, you must take over the Department!' Well, I was somewhat nonplussed, I can tell you, standing there in my dressing gown. I'd have turned it down, but I thought, no, this'll reach His Majesty's ears, and

go on my service record besides. [. . .] 'Very well,
gentlemen,' I said, 'I accept the post, I'll take it on,' I said,
only I won't stand for any nonsense, d'you hear? I've got my
eye on you lot, so watch out!' And that's just what happened,
but God, every time I walked through that department,
you'd have thought an earthquake had struck, they were
shaking in their shoes, believe me. I don't stand for any
funny business, no, not me. I put the fear of God into that
lot. Even His Majesty's Privy Council's frightened of me.
And so they should be. That's the kind of man I am. I don't
care who they are, I'll say it to anybody, 'I'm my own man,
Sir, so there!' I'm here, there, and everywhere. I drive to the
palace every day. And tomorrow, would you believe, they're
making me a Field-Marshal . . . **99**

GLOSSARY

Pushkin the greatest of Russian poets (1799–1837)

An Enemy of the People

Henrik Ibsen (1882), *trans. Arthur Miller*

WHO ☞ *Dr Stockmann, medical officer of the local baths. Decried as the 'enemy' of the title. 30s plus.*

WHERE ☞ *A room in house of the editor of the local paper, being used as a public meeting place, in a Norwegian town.*

TO WHOM ☞ *Local dignitaries, businessmen, townsfolk and his brother.*

WHEN ☞ *Contemporary with authorship.*

WHAT HAS JUST HAPPENED ☞ *Stockmann lives with his wife and young family in a small resort where his brother is Mayor, Chief Constable and Chairman of the Baths committee. Everyone is convinced the baths will bring fame and prosperity to all; every local person's life will be enriched. But Stockmann, whilst researching an article for the local paper, has found out for sure what he has long suspected; there is sewage pollution in the springs that feed the bath, caused by the local tannery. Yet his story has been deliberately lost as fear grows for the economic repercussions of the truth. So he takes his case to a public meeting. Stockmann is self-important, unpopular, righteous but brave; and has just been told that the people, that is the majority, disagree with his findings.*

WHAT HE WANTS/OBJECTIVES TO PLAY ☞

- *To impress upon those gathered the need to evolve and prove themselves as a society, what he terms 'a People'. To understand this is a term which cannot be bestowed automatically, but can only come as a result of collective work.*

- *To inspire a morality and a sense of common responsibility.*

- *To appeal to their common sense.*

- *To assert his intellectual and humanitarian authority whilst teaching them.*

Stockmann

❝ Tonight I was struck by a sudden flash of light, a discovery second to none. But before I tell it to you – a little story. I put in a good many years in the north of our country. Up there the rulers of the world are the great seal and the gigantic squadrons of duck. Man lives on ice, huddled together in little piles of stones. His whole life consists of grubbing for food. Nothing more. He can barely speak his own language. And it came to me one day that it was romantic and sentimental for a man of my education to be tending these people. They had not yet reached the stage where they needed a doctor. If the truth were to be told, a veterinary would be more in order. [. . .]

Just because there is a mass of organisms with the human shape, they do not automatically become a People! That honour has to be earned! Nor does one automatically become a man by having human shape, and living in a house, and feeding one's face – and agreeing with one's neighbours. That name also has to be earned. Now, when I came to my conclusions abut the springs – [. . .]

When I became convinced of my theory about the water, the authorities moved in at once, and I said to myself, I will fight them to the death, because – [. . .]

Let me finish. I thought to myself: the majority, I have the majority! And let me tell you, friends, it was a grand feeling. Because that's the reason I came back to this place of my birth. I wanted to give my education to this town. I loved it so, I spent months without pay or encouragement and dreamed up the whole project of the springs. And why? Not as my brother says, so that fine carriages could crowd our streets, but so that we might cure the sick, so that we might meet people from all over the world and learn from them, and become broader and more civilised. In other words, more like Men, more like A People. [. . .]

I am a revolutionist! I am in revolt against the age-old lie that the majority is always right! [. . .]

Was the majority right when they stood by while Jesus was crucified? Was the majority right when they refused to believe that the earth moved around the sun and let Galileo be driven to his knees like a dog? It takes fifty years for the majority to be right. The majority is never right until it *does* right. **99**

Ivanov

Anton Chekhov (1887), *adapt. David Hare*

WHO ☞ *Ivanov (pronounced Ee-var-noff), a regional councillor and estate owner. 30s.*

WHERE ☞ *A drawing-room in Sasha's family home, in a province in central Russia.*

TO WHOM ☞ *Sasha, his fiancée.*

WHEN ☞ *Contemporary with authorship.*

WHAT HAS JUST HAPPENED ☞ *Ivanov is a young estate owner, heavily in debt. He used to be energetic, creative, unconventional, the 'star' of the local gentry. But for the last year he has been suffering with the most profound depression. His wife Anna has just died a slow death from TB. He could not shake off his depression sufficiently to even be kind to her in her last weeks. His wife knew he was seeing Sasha: he didn't disguise his need to go over to where she lived, and the knowledge certainly precipitated her death. Both his wife and Sasha have been unfailingly supportive and loving towards Ivanov, but he seems to have lost the ability to reciprocate, and this terrifies him. He is full of loathing for how he treated Anna, and full of fear for how he will transform this relationship with Sasha into something rotten too. This is the day Ivanov was to have married Sasha. He has just burst into her home – he should have been in the church: Sasha knows what is coming. They have been left alone.*

WHAT HE WANTS / OBJECTIVES TO PLAY ☞

- *To try to explain the reality of his depression.*
- *To irrevocably separate from her.*
- *To explain the disengagement in terms of her own benefit; his path is self-destructive – she will be destroyed along with him.*
- *To communicate his very real love for her and consequently his equally real terror that she will be brought down by him.*

Ivanov

" Do you know what it feels like? To watch yourself wither? To know you have gone on living too long? To look up at the sun and see it still shining? It shines regardless. To look at an ant, carrying its burden. Even an ant can be happy with its lot. To look round, to see people's faces – this person thinks I'm a phoney. Another one pities me. Another one thinks I need help! And worst of all, to catch people listening respectfully, as if by listening they could actually learn! People think there's something deep about despair. But there isn't. As if I could found a new religion, and impart some earth-shattering truth. I still have some pride. As I came here, laughing at my own absurdity, it seemed to me the birds and the trees were beginning to laugh at me too.

[SASHA. This isn't rage. This is madness.]

Madness? This is cold sanity. Yes, the rage is speaking. But the rage tells the truth. You and I . . . we're in love, but we cannot marry. I have a perfect right to destroy my own life, but I have no right to destroy other people's. Yes. And that's what I did to my first wife. By my endless complaining. And now it's the same with you. Since we met, you've stopped laughing. You've aged. You look five years older. Your father who once was at peace with the world now stands round in confusion. Lost. The only thing I have ever wanted: to try to be honest! To try to tell the truth. And the effect has been to spread dissatisfaction around me wherever I go. I spread contagion. Everywhere I spread my contempt. As if I was doing life a favour by consenting to be alive! Oh, let me be damned in hell.

[SASHA. Do you not see? This is the moment I've longed for.
IVANOV. Why?
SASHA. This is the step you're now ready to take. At last, here, today, before this wedding, you see your condition clearly. You see it and you resolve to start a new life.
IVANOV. A new life?
SASHA. Yes.
IVANOV How? How can I? I am at the end.

SASHA. You're nowhere near the end.
IVANOV. I've done it! I'm finished.
SASHA. Keep your voice down! The guests . . .
IVANOV. Finished!
SASHA. We have to go to the church.]

The road I am on leads one way, and one way only. When a man who is educated, who is healthy – I'm by no means stupid – when a man like me starts on this path, then he's like a child wrapped in a blanket, who finds himself rolling downhill. What can stop me? What? I can't drink, wine gives me a headache. Write rotten poetry? I can't. I won't. I'm not willing to take my condition and somehow elevate it into something poetic. If I do that it's the end. I've always known the value of things. I call laziness laziness. The word for weakness is weakness. Oh, you say I'm not finished. I'm more finished than any man on earth.

He looks round.

We may be interrupted any moment. If you love me, do me one favour. Disown me. Disown me right now. **99**

Miss Julie
August Strindberg (1888), trans. Kenneth McLeish

WHO ☞ *Jean, 30-year-old manservant to His Lordship.*

WHERE ☞ *In the kitchen of a country estate in Sweden.*

TO WHOM ☞ *Miss Julie, the 25-year-old daughter of His Lordship.*

WHEN ☞ *Midsummer Night, contemporary with authorship.*

WHAT HAS JUST HAPPENED ☞ *It is past midnight and Jean is still not off duty but is spending Midsummer Night in the kitchen, in the presence of the somewhat wild Miss Julie. This night marks an important festival in Sweden, a time of national rejoicing, a 24-hour Saturnalia when social barriers are swept aside and everyone enjoys a holiday. Having broken off her engagement with her fiancé, Julie has been throwing herself at Jean, despite being his social superior. He is more than a match for her and they have been undoubtedly enjoying each other's company – albeit sado-masochistically. Though a servant, he is aware of the hold he has over her, and aware too that she is vulnerable. Cruel, ambitious, and a cynical opportunist, Jean intends to have sex with her, and embarks on this story, which we later learn he has mostly invented, to win her over. The speech begins as he admits, following prompting by Julie, that he was in love years ago . . . with her.*

WHAT HE WANTS/OBJECTIVES TO PLAY ☞

- *To lure her into a trap, offering himself as a friend, and as an equal, to get her into bed.*

- *To seduce her and draw compassion and pity from her by turn.*

- *To appeal to her sense of the poetic and the dramatic and to the ideal of the 'noble savage' which, he knows, she believes in.*

- *To climb the first rung of the ladder to a life outside of this servitude by seducing her.*

Jean

❝ It was ridiculous. That's why I didn't want to tell, before. But now I'd better. You know what the world looks like from the bottom – no, of course you don't. Hawks, falcons – they soar above us, most of the time; who sees their backs? I lived in a cottage; seven brothers and sisters; a pig; wasteland all round, not even a tree. But out of the window I could see all the wall of His Lordship's estate. Apple trees, on the other side. The Garden of Eden . . . angel-guardians, swords of fire . . . Mind you, they didn't stop us, me and the other boys. The Tree of Life. You don't approve . . .

[MISS JULIE. All boys steal apples.
JEAN. You say that but you still don't approve.]

Too late now. One day I went into the garden, with my mother, to weed the onions. Not far from the vegetable garden, in the jasmine bushes, was a Turkish pavilion, covered in honeysuckle. I'd no idea what it was for, but it was beautiful. People went in, came out . . . and one day someone left the door open. I peeped in. Pictures of kings and emperors . . . scarlet curtains, tassels . . . you know. I –

He breaks off a lilac twig and holds it for her to smell.

I'd never been in the Big House, never been anywhere but church, and this was far more magnificent. I couldn't stop thinking about it. All I wanted, just once, was to enjoy it, revel in it – *enfin*, one day I crept in, stood there gaping. Someone was coming! For fine folk, there was only one way in or out. But I found another, and did I use it!

Miss Julie has taken the lilac, and now lets it fall on the table.

As soon as I got out, I ran, through the raspberries, across the strawberries, into the rose-garden. There was someone there: a pink frock, white stockings; it was you. I dived into a compost heap. Think of it: thistles, mud, stink. I watched you walking in the rose-garden, and I thought how crazy it was that a thief could go to heaven and mix with angels, but a peasant like me couldn't go to the Big House garden and play with his Lordship's daughter.

[MISS JULIE (*mocking; sentimentally*). Imagine! If all poor peasants could think like that!
JEAN (*ironically at first, then seriously*). Oh, they do. They do.
MISS JULIE. Being Poor – how dreadful.]

(*Really serious.*) See, your ladyship, a dog can stretch out on your Ladyship's shoulder, a horse can feel your hand stroking him, but a servant – (*New tone.*) Oh, now and then someone forces his way up in the world. Not often. Anyway, d'you know what I did next? Jumped into the mill-stream with all my clothes on. They fished me out, thrashed me. Next Sunday, when my father and all the others were going to Granny's, I worked it so I could stay at home. I washed myself with soap, hot water, put on my Sunday best and went to church – to see you. And when I saw you, I decided to die, on the spot. But painlessly, happily. I suddenly remembered, if you sleep under an elder tree, it's fatal. There was a big one, just in bloom. I tore off all the flowers, made a bed of them in the oat-bin and lay there. Oats: have you ever noticed how smooth they are, smooth as human skin . . . Never mind, I pulled the lid shut, closed my eyes and slept. I was really ill, but as you see, I didn't die. I don't know what I wanted. You? No chance. You stood for everything I could never have, the gulf between what I wanted and what I was. **99**

A Woman of No Importance

Oscar Wilde (1893)

WHO ☞   *Gerald Arbuthnot, a young gentleman, 20s.*

WHERE ☞   *The Hall at Hunstanton Chase.*

TO WHOM ☞   *His mother, Mrs Arbuthnot.*

WHEN ☞   *Contemporary with authorship.*

WHAT HAS JUST HAPPENED ☞   *Among the guests at Hunstanton Chase are the opinionated and vivacious American Hester Worsley and the eager Gerald Arbuthnot who delights hostess Lady Hunstanton with the news that he is to become secretary to the charming but selfish bachelor Lord Illingworth. But when Gerald's normally reticent mother, Mrs Arbuthnot, appears, she discourages his ambition, though she cannot forbid it. What Gerald doesn't know, and what his mother does, is that Lord Illingworth is actually his father!*

WHAT HE WANTS/OBJECTIVES TO PLAY ☞

- *To earn his mother's love and support.*

- *To put the case forward in emotional as well as practical terms.*

- *To challenge all that his mother stands for – and to separate his views from hers.*

- *To make her feel she has held him back in the past.*

- *To imagine the opportunities he believes his new position and elevated status will bring him, including the chance to woo Hester Worsley.*

Gerald Arbuthnot

" Mother, how changeable you are! You don't seem to know your own mind for a single moment. An hour and a half ago in the drawing-room you agreed to the whole thing; now you turn round and make objections, and try to force me to give up my one chance in life. Yes, my one chance. You don't suppose that men like Lord Illingworth are to be found every day, do you, mother? It is very strange that when I have had such a wonderful piece of good luck, the one person to put difficulties in my way should be my own mother. Besides, you know, mother, I love Hester Worsley. Who could help loving her? I love her more than I ever have told you, far more. And if I had a position, if I had prospects, I could – I could ask her to . . . Don't you understand now, mother, what it means to me to be Lord Illingworth's secretary? To start like that is to find a career ready for one – before one – waiting for one. If I were Lord Illingworth's secretary I could ask Hester to be my wife. As a wretched bank clerk with a hundred a year it would be an impertinence.

[MRS ARBUTHNOT. I fear you need have no hopes of Miss Worsley. I know her views on life. She has told them to me. (*A pause.*)]

Then I have my ambition left, at any rate. That is something – I am glad I have that! You have always tried to crush my ambition, mother – haven't you? You have told me that the world is a wicked place, that success is not worth having, that society is shallow, and all that sort of thing – well, I don't believe it, mother. I think the world must be delightful. I think society must be exquisite. I think success is a thing worth having. You have been wrong in all that you taught me, mother, quite wrong. Lord Illingworth is a successful man. He is a fashionable man. He is a man who lives in the world and for it. Well, I would give anything to be just like Lord Illingworth. **"**

The Seagull

Anton Chekhov (1896), trans. Stephen Mulrine

WHO ☞ *Trigorin, a middle-aged successful writer, partner of Arkadina, 40s.*

WHERE ☞ *On a croquet lawn, in the midday heat. On the estate of Arkadina's brother.*

TO WHOM ☞ *Nina, the young daughter of a local wealthy landowner, early 20s.*

WHEN ☞ *Contemporary with authorship.*

WHAT HAS JUST HAPPENED ☞ *Kostya, Arkadina's son and a failed dramatist, has just hurried off from Nina, the object of his affections, having been interrupted by Trigorin. Trigorin is making a secret study of all the people on the estate and their relationships; his interest in Nina is purely forensic, as the love interest for his lover's son. Nina is evidently enthralled by Trigorin: she has been pressing him for information on how it is to be a celebrity, to be famous, to be successful. Trigorin responds in this speech to her line 'But you have a marvellous life!'.*

WHAT HE WANTS/OBJECTIVES TO PLAY ☞

- *To get this torment off his chest: it is as if he has never said any of this out loud.*

- *To make her aware that she is naive and wrong about him. His life is neither brilliant nor interesting, just pressurised constantly.*

- *To be understood.*

Trigorin

❝ What's so great about it? (*Looks at his watch.*) I've got to do some writing now. I'm sorry, but I've no time . . . (*Laughs.*) You've touched me on a sore spot, as they say, and

I'm starting to get heated now, and slightly irritated. Yes, all right, let's have a talk. Let's talk about my wonderful, brilliant life. Where shall we begin? (*Thinks for a moment.*) You know, some people have what's termed an *idée fixe* – for example, when a person thinks about nothing but the moon, day and night. Well, I have my own moon. Day and night I'm obsessed with one compelling thought: I must write, I must write, I must . . . No sooner have I finished one novel than I've got to write another, I don't know why, then a third, and after that a fourth. I write incessantly, without a break, I can't help it. So what's wonderful and brilliant about that, eh? It's a hellish life. Here I am with you, I feel excited and happy, yet at the same time, I can't get it out of my mind that I have an unfinished novel waiting for me. I look at that cloud there, shaped like a grand piano. And I think: I'll have to mention that somewhere in a story, that a cloud floated by, shaped like a piano. And there's a scent of heliotrope. So I make another mental note: sickly-sweet perfume, colour of widow's weeds, use it in a description of a summer evening. I try to catch every word, every phrase that passes between us, and quickly lock all these words and phrases away in my literary larder: they might come in handy! When I stop work, I dash off to the theatre or go fishing – I should be able to relax, forget everything, but no! There's a heavy iron ball already on the move in my head – a new subject, and it's dragging me back to my desk, so I've got to hurry and start writing again. It's like that all the time, I give myself no peace. I feel as if I'm devouring my own life: that in order to deliver honey to someone out there somewhere, I have to gather pollen from all my finest flowers, then tear those same flowers up by the roots and trample on them. I must be mad, surely? I mean, do my family and friends treat me like a normal person? 'What are you writing now?' 'What have you got in store for us?' It's always the same, it never stops, and I have the distinct feeling that all the attention they pay me, all that praise and admiration, is nothing but a sham. I'm being deceived, the way people deceive a sick man, and occasionally I have this fear that someone will steal up from behind and

grab me, then whisk me off to an asylum, like Gogol's
madman. In my young days, when I was at my best, just
starting out, writing was a form of torture. A minor writer,
particularly if he's not having much luck, feels clumsy and
awkward, no use to anybody. He's on edge the whole time, a
bag of nerves. He's irresistibly drawn to people involved in
literature and the arts, he hangs around them unrecognised
and unnoticed, afraid to look anybody in the eye, like a
compulsive gambler with no money. I couldn't see my
readers, but somehow I thought of them as hostile and
sceptical. I was afraid of audiences, really terrified.
Whenever I had a new play staged, I would imagine all the
dark-haired people hated it, and the fair-haired people
couldn't care less! It was absolutely dreadful. Sheer
torture! **99**

GLOSSARY

Gogol's madman i.e. the subject of Gogol's story 'Notes of a Madman'
    (1835)

To Damascus Part III

August Strindberg (1900), *trans. Michael Meyer*

WHO ☞   *Tempter: any age.*

WHERE ☞   *In a beautifully panelled dining room.*

TO WHOM ☞   *Stranger.*

WHEN ☞   *A mythical past and a contemporary present: this is an expressionistic play and non-definable in its time setting.*

WHAT HAS JUST HAPPENED ☞   *This play is the story of a man, known simply as Stranger, who, having led a fairly dissolute and dishonourable life, makes amends and is journeying to a monastery to begin a life of humble contrition. In order to do that, he has to say goodbye to all that binds him, including people. Stranger has just reunited – and again broken up with – his first wife. It is an illustration of how they could not even be friends in their previous life together, let alone with a second chance in this new reality. The figure of Tempter is a rogue/alter-ego to Stranger – there to test and probe Stranger's responses to the interactions with these people from his life. Stranger has just asked him why his, Tempter's, marriage failed. He offers this as a response.*

WHAT HE WANTS/OBJECTIVES TO PLAY ☞

- *To make Stranger feel fine about not hitting it off – again – with his first wife; in fact to fan the flames of his strength of feeling against her.*

- *To support Stranger's misogynist tendencies.*

- *To collude with Stranger, engaging with him in such a way as to suggest they are both familiar with the 'weird world of women'.*

Tempter

❝ Well, you know how a man marries to have a home to come home to, and a woman so as to get out. She wanted to get out, and I wanted to get in. I was so constituted that I couldn't go out with her because I felt she was soiled by other men's glances. In company, my wonderful wife became a grimacing little marmoset whom I couldn't bear to look at. So, I had to stay at home. And then, she stayed away. And when I saw her next, she was another person. She, my white virgin parchment, was scrawled with crows' feet; her lovely clear features were distorted into reflections of the satyr-masks of other men; in her eyes I saw miniature photographs of bull-fighters and hussars. In her voice I heard the strange tones of strangers' voices; on our piano, which hitherto had known only classical harmonies, she now strummed strangers' jangling trivia; our table was littered with the literary choice of strangers. To sum up, my whole existence was perverted into a spiritual concubinage with men I had never met – which was against my nature, which has always craved women. And – need I say it? – the taste of these strange gentlemen was always diametrically opposed to my own. She developed a positive genius for sniffing out what I detested. She called it 'protecting her personality'. Can you understand that?

[STRANGER. I understand it, but I wouldn't try to explain.]

And yet this woman swore that she loved me; and that I didn't love her. But I loved her so much that I didn't want to talk to anyone else – I felt I was being unfaithful to her if I found pleasure in anyone else's company, even a man's. I'd married to find female companionship, and to get this, I gave up my friends; I'd married to find companionship, and instead found utter loneliness. So I kept house and home to provide a female companion for men I'd never met. *C'est l'amour, mon ami.* **❞**

GLOSSARY

C'est l'amour, mon ami (French) It's love, my friend

Man and Superman

George Bernard Shaw (1903)

WHO ☞   *Don Juan, the legendary womaniser, any age.*

WHERE ☞   *In Hell.*

TO WHOM ☞   *The Devil; Dona Ana, the eternal female; and Don Gonzalo, a libertine disguised as a statue.*

WHEN ☞   *Contemporary with authorship.*

WHAT HAS JUST HAPPENED ☞   *This is taken from the third act of this play, often performed as a separate piece: a dream episode in which Don Juan and the Devil engage in a lively debate concerning the war between the sexes. Don Juan is the dream-induced alter ego of Jack Tanner, who has previously been pursued by the predatory Ann Whitefield (in the dream sequence portrayed as Dona Ana). Also present is Don Gonzalo, a libertine disguised as a statue. This speech is Don Juan's response to Dona Ana's suggestion that marriage is a necessary institution within society.*

WHAT HE WANTS/OBJECTIVES TO PLAY ☞

- *To enlighten his friends and entertain them too.*

- *To strip away all artifice and convention from the business of seduction.*

- *To broadcast his distaste and mistrust for the illogical irrelevance of a lifelong commitment within a relationship.*

- *To take apart Dona Ana's argument as unrealistic, but idealistic.*

Don Juan

❝ When I was on earth, and made those proposals to ladies which, though universally condemned, have made me so interesting a hero of legend, I was not infrequently met in some such way as this. The lady would say that she would countenance my advances, provided they were honourable. On inquiring what that proviso meant, I found that it meant that I proposed to get possession of her property if she had any, or to undertake her support for life if she had not; that I desired her continual companionship, counsel, and conversation to the end of my days, and would take a most solemn oath to be always enraptured by them: above all, that I would turn my back on all other women for ever for her sake. I did not object to these conditions because they were exorbitant and inhuman: it was their extraordinary irrelevance that prostrated me. I invariably replied with perfect frankness that I had never dreamt of any of these things; that unless the lady's character and intellect were equal or superior to my own, her conversation must degrade and her counsel mislead me; that her constant companionship might, for all I knew, become intolerably tedious to me; that I could not answer for my feelings for a week in advance, much less to the end of my life; that to cut me off from all natural and unconstrained intercourse with half my fellow creatures would narrow and warp me if I submitted to it, and, if not, would bring me under the curse of clandestinity; that, finally, my proposals to her were wholly unconnected with any of these matters, and were the outcome of a perfectly simple impulse of my manhood towards her womanhood.

[ANA. You mean that it was an immoral impulse.]

Nature, my dear lady, is what you call immoral. I blush for it; but I cannot help it. Nature is a pandar, Time a wrecker, and Death a murderer. I have always preferred to stand up to those facts and build institutions on their recognition. You prefer to propitiate the three devils by proclaiming their chastity, their thrift, and their loving kindness; and to base your institutions on these flatteries. Is it any wonder that the institutions do not work smoothly? **99**

Children of the Sun

Maxim Gorky (1905), *trans. Stephen Mulrine*

WHO ☞   *Protasov (pronounced Proh-*TAH-*soff), a landowner and amateur scientist.*

WHERE ☞   *A run-down country house in rural Russia.*

TO WHOM ☞   *His wife, sister and houseguests, made up of literary, scientific and artistic intelligentsia.*

WHEN ☞   *Contemporary with authorship.*

WHAT HAS JUST HAPPENED ☞   *The temperature for social unrest is rising on the streets, there are rumours of an approaching cholera epidemic, and it is a far from harmonious household. Protasov, though aware of the political unrest outside his home, is largely unaware of the personal tensions and intrigues within it; he is even unaware, unlike the rest of the company, that his wife is being seduced by one of the guests, an artist. He is obsessively preoccupied with his scientific experiments and with his idealistic notions of being part of a unique and revolutionary generation of visionaries. In this speech he takes the opportunity to remind those present of his dream of a radiant future for mankind.*

WHAT HE WANTS/OBJECTIVES TO PLAY ☞

- *To change the dynamic in the party: this is supposed to be a celebratory gathering of like and great minds.*

- *To teach those assembled about the potential of mankind for greatness.*

- *To identify people like themselves, liberal intellectuals as the 'children of the sun' who will lead the race out of darkness.*

- *To inspire them.*

Protasov

❝ I can see how life grows and develops, I can see it
yielding to the relentless questing of my mind, opening up
its profound and wonderful mysteries before me. I see myself
already the master of many things, and I know that man will
attain mastery over all things! Everything that grows becomes
more complex – people are constantly raising their expectations,
both of life, and of themselves. Under the sun's rays, some
insignificant and shapeless lump of protein once flared up
into life, multiplied itself, came together to form an eagle, a
lion, a human being; and there'll come a time when out of
us, mere people, out of all people, there will arise a magnificent, shapely organism – humanity! Yes, humanity, sirs! And
then every cell will contain the past – the fulfilment of our
great conquest of ideas – our work! The present will be free,
comradely labour, carried out for the sheer pleasure of that
labour, and the future – I can feel, I can see it – will be truly
wonderful. Humanity is growing and maturing. That's life,
that's what it means!

[LIZA. Oh I wish I could believe that. I wish it so much.
VAGHIN. I like you in your poetic vein.]

The fear of death – that's what stops us from becoming bold,
beautiful, free people. It hangs over us like a dark cloud,
covers the earth with shadows, out of which phantoms are
born. It causes people to stray from the direct route to
freedom, from the broad highway of experiment. It inspires
them to construct hasty and ill-conceived speculations on the
meaning of existence, it terrifies the reason, and then
thought creates fallacies! But we, people like us, the children
of the sun, of the bright source of life, we shall overcome the
dark terror of death. We are the children of the sun, yes!
That's what burns in our blood, that's what generates proud,
fiery ideas, lighting up the gloom of our confusion – the sun,
an ocean of energy and beauty, and intoxicating joy for the
soul! **❞**

Fanny's First Play

George Bernard Shaw (1911)

WHO ☞　　　　*Duvallet, late 20s plus.*

WHERE ☞　　　*The drawing room of Margaret's family home.*

TO WHOM ☞　 *Margaret's parents, in her presence.*

WHEN ☞　　　*Contemporary with authorship.*

WHAT HAS JUST HAPPENED ☞　*Duvallet is a Frenchman visiting London, who chances upon the charming Margaret in the theatre one night. They get on famously, and he invites her to a dance hall where they spend the evening just dancing and enjoying themselves. There is a police raid, where all assembled are assumed to be of loose moral virtue and in the crush to get everyone onto the street, Duvallet and Margaret get into a fight with the police. They defend themselves and are imprisoned, separately, for two weeks. On their release, she is returned to her parents, where the story shatters their world. They had no idea where she was for the two weeks, and they are stunned to discover that Duvallet, who they assume had honourable intentions toward their daughter, has none at all, though she, one suspects, has feelings for him. In fact he is married, has daughters of his own and is simply enjoying the company of such a socially and politically enlightened young woman as Margaret. He has done nothing wrong; he has not betrayed Margaret: he is one of the new classes who believe in integrity and honesty, and who despise the hypocrisy at the heart of French – and English – society. He is explaining himself to Margaret's mother in response to her question as to whether he would allow his own daughters to go out with a stranger who had no honourable intentions.*

WHAT HE WANTS/OBJECTIVES TO PLAY ☞

- *To congratulate them on their daughter, and her extraordinary qualities.*
- *To compliment them on their national characteristics.*
- *To deflect any sense of outrage or impropriety.*
- *To befriend them all.*

Duvallet

" Ah, Madam, my daughters are French girls. That is very different. It would not be correct for a French girl to go about alone and speak to men as English and American girls do. That is why I so immensely admire the English people. You are so free – so unprejudiced – your women are so brave and frank – their minds are so – how do you say? – wholesome. I intend to have my daughters educated in England. Nowhere else in the world but in England could I have met at a Variety Theatre a charming young lady of perfect respectability, and enjoyed a dance with her at a public dancing saloon. And where else are women trained to box and knock out the teeth of policemen as a protest against injustice and violence? (*Rising with immense élan.*) Your daughter, Madam, is superb. Your country is a model to the rest of Europe. If you were a Frenchman, stifled with prudery, hypocrisy and the tyranny of the family and the home, you would understand how an enlightened Frenchman admires and envies your freedom, your broadmindedness, and the fact that home life can hardly be said to exist in England. You have made an end of the despotism of the parent; the family council is unknown to you; everywhere in these islands one can enjoy the exhilarating, the soul-liberating spectacle of men quarrelling with their brothers, defying their fathers, and refusing to speak to their mothers. In France we are not men: we are only sons – grown-up children. Here one is a human being – an end in himself. [. . .]

Sir: if all Frenchwomen were like your daughter – if all Frenchmen had the good sense, the power of seeing things as they really are, the calm judgement, the open mind, the philosophic grasp, the foresight and true courage, which are so natural to you as an Englishman that you are hardly conscious of possessing them, France would become the greatest nation in the world. "

Heartbreak House

George Bernard Shaw (1919)

WHO ☞   *Alfred Mangan, 40s plus.*

WHERE ☞   *The drawing room.*

TO WHOM ☞   *Ellie, his younger fiancée.*

WHEN ☞   *Contemporary with authorship.*

WHAT HAS JUST HAPPENED ☞   *Ellie is planning to marry the millionaire and much older Mangan in order to save her idealistic, wholly good but totally impractical father from penury. Though her family knows she does not love him, they have embraced Mangan as the saviour of their very lives. She is invited, with Mangan, to a house party of the father of a close friend – the house of the title. After dinner Mangan and Ellie retire to the drawing room and he explains to her, rather viciously, that it was he who ruined her father. He is not the benign benefactor who appears to be keeping the old man in a job after the collapse of his business; instead he engineered the collapse of that business to begin with.*

WHAT HE WANTS/OBJECTIVES TO PLAY ☞

- *To rudely waken her to his true nature and character.*
- *To alienate her, and so maybe release himself from the contractual obligation.*
- *To be free of the burden he has been carrying for some time now.*
- *To instruct her in the ways of capitalism, highlighting her ignorance up to this point.*
- *To belittle her father, knowing that this will cut her to the core.*

Alfred Mangan

❝ Of course you don't understand: what do you know about business? You just listen and learn. Your father's business was a new business; and I don't start new businesses: I let other fellows start them. They put all their money and their friends' money into starting them. They wear out their souls and bodies trying to make a success of them. They're what you call enthusiasts. But the first dead lift of the thing is too much for them: and they haven't enough financial experience. In a year or so they have either to let the whole show go bust, or sell out to a new lot of fellows for a few deferred ordinary shares: that is if they're lucky enough to get anything at all. As likely as not the very same thing happens to the new lot. They put in more money and a couple of years more work; and then perhaps they have to sell out to a third lot. If it's really a big thing the third lot will have to sell out too, and leave their work and their money behind them. And that's where the real businessman comes in: where I come in. But I'm cleverer than some: I don't mind dropping a little money to start the process. I took your father's measure. I saw that he had a sound idea, and that he would work himself silly for it if he got the chance. I saw that he was a child in business, and was dead certain to outrun his expenses and be in too great a hurry to wait for his market. I knew that the surest way to ruin a man who doesn't know how to handle money is to give him some. I explained my idea to some friends in the city, and they found the money; for I take no risks in ideas, even when they're my own. Your father and the friends that ventured their money with him were no more to me than a heap of squeezed lemons. You've been wasting your gratitude: my kind heart is all rot. I'm sick of it. When I see your father beaming at me with his moist, grateful eyes, regularly wallowing in gratitude, I sometimes feel I must tell him the truth or burst. What stops me is that I know he wouldn't believe me. He'd think it was my modesty, as you did just now. He'd think anything rather than the truth, which is that he's a blamed fool, and that I am a man that knows how to take care of himself.

Now what do you think of me? **99**

1407